ISLAND OF TEARS,
ISLAND OF HOPE

VISAYAN SEA

PANAY

ILOILO

GUIMARAS STRAIT

Cadiz

Silay

Bacolod

BAGO

La CARLOTA

KANLA-ON

PANAY GULF

HINIGARAN

BINALBAGAN

BATANG

HIMAMAYLAN

KABANKALAN

DANCALAN

TABUGON • ORINGAD

SIPALAY • MAGBALLO

NEGROS

HINOBA-AN

Dumaguete

CEBU

Cebu

TANON STRAIT

BOHOL STRAIT

South China Sea

Philippine Sea

BAGUIO

Manila

LUZON

MINDORO

SAMAR

CEBU

Sulu Sea

LEYTE

PALAWAN

PANAY

NEGROS

BOHOL

MINDANAO

PHILIPPINE ISLANDS

ISLAND OF TEARS, ISLAND OF HOPE

*Living the Gospel
in a Revolutionary Situation*

Niall O'Brien

ORBIS BOOKS

Maryknoll, New York 10545

Copyright © 1993 by Niall O'Brien
Published by Orbis Books, Maryknoll, NY 10545
All rights reserved
Manufactured in the United States of America

Photograph on page 2 courtesy of *Fellowship Magazine*. Photograph on page 215
by Niall O'Brien. Cover and all other photographs by Ed Gerlock, © 1993. Used
with permission.

Library of Congress Cataloging-in-Publication Data

O'Brien, Niall.
    Island of tears, island of hope : living the Gospel in a
revolutionary situation / Niall O'Brien.
        p.   cm.
    Includes bibliographical references and index.
    ISBN 0-88344-927-7
    1. Catholic Church—Missions—Philippines—History—20th century.
2. O'Brien, Niall.   3. Missionaries—Philippines—Negros Island—
Biography.   4. Missionaries—Ireland—Biography.   5. Nonviolence—
Religious aspects—Catholic Church.   6. Basic Christian
communities—Philippines.   7. Philippines—Politics and
government—1986-   8. Negros Island (Philippines)—Politics and
government.   I. Title.
BV3380.O37   1993
282'.5995—dc20
                                                        93-23776
                                                        CIP

For

Bishop Antonio Y. Fortich

A great Filipino,
a noble and wise Churchman,
a Christian who taught us that
the path to holiness in Negros
must lie through the cane fields.
He took that path himself.

Contents

PART III
GRASP THE BARBED WIRE
A Spirituality for Active Nonviolence

Foreword

While reading Fr. Niall O'Brien's challenging book about the people of Negros I was filled with deep gratitude and hope. It confirms in me the insight that, in mysterious but very concrete ways, poor and often persecuted Christians in different parts of the Third World have rediscovered and are teaching us, in the rich countries, the deepest truth of the gospel: liberation and new life through identification with the Suffering Servant of Isaiah, with the Suffering Servant Jesus Christ.

In Brazil, the movement of the Suffering Servant grew up among the poorest of the poor, those for whom life makes no sense because it is mere suffering. Hundreds of thousands in the Christian Basic Communities are living out of the same perspective. They would affirm: "We are the Suffering Servants; we have heard that we are called to set free and reconcile the *whole* people; we have accepted the call; we are trying to shake off our fears and our submission; we are standing up for justice. Like the Suffering Servant Jesus we accept the consequences of our speaking the truth through life and deeds even to the gift of our life. We do not reply to lie with lie, to violence with violence, to revenge with revenge, but we resist with firmness (*firmeza permanente*, "active nonviolence"). Thus we transform our suffering into a liberating power for ourselves and for the "others" — the persecutors, the rich, the indifferent. They believe that the renewed Church and the renewed society, obtained through this power, will permit life in greater justice and in dignity for all and open the possibility for forgiveness and reconciliation.

From Brazil to Africa, to Bangladesh, Burma, China and to the Philippines stretches the large family of humble people —

Christians, Muslims, Hindus, Buddhists, who are discovering this liberating force of nonviolence as they are about to build new societies aimed at justice, participation, and peace. This "people power" proves to be truly revolutionary in our world as we enter the twenty-first century. This powerful and increasingly more organized strength from below, which puts absolute respect and trust into the human being, is surely a great sign of hope in the midst of the tremendous destructive forces of greed, economic exploitation and militarism that dominate the world.

Fr. Niall O'Brien has pursued this thread of hope in a unique way in the Philippines and more specially in the sugar island of Negros. His personal experience of suffering persecution and imprisonment permits him to be an authentic witness. Based upon a profound insight into the situation, he does not shy away from the crucial and most controversial issues. On the contrary, he helps us, out of the historic background, to understand better the position of each group: the landlords, the military, the NPA-guerrilla forces, the Church, as well as of the poor, suffering people. His insight helps us to understand better the structure of injustice and the violence inherent in it, but it also provides the key to liberation work rooted in gospel nonviolence.

His highlighting of the *passivity* of the population of the Philippines in general — fruit of centuries of oppression — is one of the most important themes of the book. By working to overcome this passivity through "people power" the old choice between passive subordination and armed resistance is challenged by the third possibility — nonviolent lifestyle and combat for justice. From this theme then, he develops different strands of hope of overcoming traditions of revenge, resignation, exploitation and military domination. The opportunity opens to rediscover the human and the divine in the "other."

It will be of help to many who are searching for a way to commit themselves in the struggle for liberation that Fr. Niall O'Brien deals in detail with the gospel message of nonviolence and the Church's teaching on the justified use of violence. If we want to choose the means of liberation proposed by our God of Justice, Love, Truth and Pardon we have to know Jesus' radical message of nonviolence as well as the groping for solutions and the deep divisions existing in the tradition of the Catholic Church in dealing with this essential issue. The humble people, who know little theology, easily discover in Jesus the nonviolent liberator and try to live out this life-giving power, while theologians and Church leaders, often linked to and submitting to those in power or unaware of the power of the nonviolent way of God, are still clinging to the "use of violence as a last resort." Even though there is visible progress toward the nonviolent position, the lack of clear, unambiguous leadership on the part of the Catholic Church for peaceful solutions has been the cause of endless conflicts of conscience and of the failure of the Church to be the light on the mountain leading to mature, peaceful overcoming of injustice and all forms of violence.

This book truly bears the mark of the wisdom of Fr. Niall O'Brien's life experience. This is apparent not only in the many touching and significant stories recounted, but also and very specially in his helpful advice of how to work patiently, in a reflective and persevering way, for nonviolent change. This gives guidance and support to those "on the way." Niall O'Brien is so close to the Suffering Servants of Negros in the Christian Base Communities that he carries with them their cross and rejoices in their unwavering belief that in the end life — God — is stronger than injustice and death.

Finally, as one reads through these pages, the image of a great Suffering Servant of Negros, Bishop Fortich, evolves more and more clearly. To me, this pastor, who has listened, learned, and grown, who has been transformed by the suffering people of Negros, and who has never ceased to dialogue with all involved in the conflict, is a powerful sign of hope for the future — a visible sign for what is possible!

Out of the darkest and most depressing situations people are awakened by God to be the witnesses and prophets embracing the nonviolent way that leads from captivity to freedom.

HILDEGARD GOSS-MAYR

Acknowledgments

This story follows the journey of a people toward freedom, while the author struggles along behind. I am grateful to the people of Negros for allowing me to accompany them and I ask their forgiveness that I am so slow to learn.

The names of certain people and places have been altered in this book to protect the safety and confidences of some and because of the feelings of the families of others.

The monetary value ascribed to the peso is the value it had in dollars at the time of a particular event. Since the dates of those events differ, so do the values ascribed to the peso.

The Bible quotations are taken from the Christian Community Bible except for Romans 14:17-19 and Matthew 23:2-3 which are from the New American Bible.

For help in producing this book, I thank Tadgh McDonnell and Mila Abrera. For reading the manuscript and making helpful suggestions, I thank Dennis Murphy, Hildegard Goss-Mayr, Sr. Xavier Marie Bual and Bernard Cleary. For substantial help with the bibliography and notes I thank Simon Peter Gregorio.

A special thanks is due to Rowena Sumande, Joy Hofilena Gepes and Rali Dioneo who worked so hard on the typing.

Finally, without the inspiration, encouragement and painstaking work of Robert Ellsberg this book would not have seen the light of day. He conceived the idea and stayed with me through all the labor pains till the moment of birth.

This book tells only part of the story; space did not allow me to introduce you to so many people who have been working to make Negros a better place and who are still quietly working away without any fanfare. Their story is written not in books but in lives of the people.

N. O'B.
Negros, Philippines
January 1993

PART I

ISLAND OF TEARS

[1]

Island of Tears

February 1986

Old women, young women, nuns in habits, students, people from every walk of life stood, sat and knelt before the approaching armored tanks. They sang, they prayed, they trembled — a trembling wall of flesh before a moving wall of steel.

Those who knew Marcos over the years knew his record of deceit, of secret murders and assassinations; they knew the standard operating procedure of torture by his interrogators. His army had committed atrocities and massacres. Escalante, in the island of Negros, where unarmed demonstrators had been mowed down a few months before, was fresh in everyone's mind. That was why the people trembled, fearing bombs from above and shells and relentless steel treads from in front.

But this time it was different. Those tanks halted before the massive faith of thousands and thousands of unarmed people. And from all over the world full half of the human race watched from moment to moment for nearly three full days till those menacing helicopters overhead stalled, turned back or defected. They watched from every city of the world, from Nairobi and Paris, from Rio and Belfast and East Berlin and Prague. Especially from East Berlin and Prague. But they also watched from Beijing, and they sensed that this was more momentous in its own way than that first footstep on the moon.

3

I watched from my cousin's house in New Jersey. I also held a small shortwave radio in my hand and followed a separate report from the British Broadcasting Corporation from Manila. During the night I awoke at intervals and tuned into the BBC. It was about 7:12 A.M., a few minutes after they had finished the news, when the announcer interrupted the next program to say that President Marcos had fled and was on a U.S. helicopter heading for Hawaii. It was only at that moment that I was sure I would be going back—back to the island of Negros in the central Philippines.

José, Lilly, Nonoi

The island of Negros, situated about three hundred miles south of Manila, is the fifth largest island in the Philippine archipelago. About the size of Holland, it is shaped like a bulky Christmas stocking. It has a spine of high volcanic mountains down its eastern side, leaving a wide, rich plain on the western side where most of its three and a quarter million people live. Ninety percent of that rich plain is covered with sugar cane. When you say Negros you say sugar.

I returned to the Philippines in January 1987, just before the referendum for a new post-Marcos constitution, and almost immediately I flew down to the island of Negros, landing in Bacolod, the capital city of western Negros.

Bacolod had changed. Its streets were dirty and neglected; its buildings unpainted and dilapidated. Few cars were on the streets; you could park anywhere. At night the street lights were dim and the streets themselves were empty by 8 P.M. The bishop's palace had been burned down, and only a dark hulk stood where welcoming lights used to greet visitors; there were beggars where no beggars had been before. With the fall of Marcos and the fall of the price of sugar, the city was in decline.

At least the cathedral had not changed. That massive pile of Spanish faith still dominated the center of the city, looking out over the plaza. I walked along, startled at first by the graffiti on the walls — strange graffiti, *educated* graffiti — saying that Bishop Antonio Fortich was a communist and his priests akin to terrorists.

A few hundred yards from where I now walked stood the Bacolod provincial jail where I and my companions had spent some time, accused of murdering our town mayor and his bodyguards. That attempt to discredit the work of the Church had failed but, nonetheless, we had been expelled from the Philippines; only the end of the old regime made it possible for us to return there now. Returning was sweet and yet sad.

A cry from the street stopped me. A man pushing a cart full of charcoal and looking pretty dusty himself was waving to me. He had curly hair and a big, broad smile. I approached. Someone from my old parish in the mountains? Someone from the sugar plantation where I had lived for several years? He could see I was groping.

"Don't you remember me, Padre? José Garcia. I was in the next cell to you when you were in prison." We embraced warmly, then José stood back and told me that I looked great after two years away. Then he asked me to come over to his house, which was only a few hundred yards from where we stood, to see his wife and child.

The house — well, it was more of a shack — was small but in its own way cozy, one inner room and an attached balcony affair, all made from bamboos and reeds. Dinah, his wife, proudly showed me their baby girl, Andrea, and the banana trees and the native vegetables they had planted around.

Theirs was a strange story: José and Dinah had farmed a little plot in the mountains of Hinoba-an in the south of the island. Thousands of peasants had done this in a search for independence and escape from the plantations in the lowlands. Then one day José was arrested on a charge of illegal logging and was kept permanently in the prison in Hinoba-an town without the case ever coming to court. Gradually he was detailed duties around the prison and allowed to live in the compound and not in the cell. Dinah moved in with him. He brought the other prisoners their food and ran messages for the guards.

José's real trouble began one night when he was awakened and asked to dig a grave and help to bury some dead bodies. With horror he told Dinah what had happened. He was sure that the bodies were those of some prisoners who had disappeared and were supposed to have escaped; these were prisoners he had brought food to. A while later the same thing happened; again he was called in the night to bury prisoners who had been summarily executed by the military without trial. The families came weeping and looking for them and were told that they had escaped to the mountains and had probably joined the New Peoples Army—the armed wing of the communist party. José and Dinah were filled with fear.

Then one day José was asked to go up the mountains to help harvest some of the chief of police's corn. Dinah had heard that this was just a ploy to get rid of José: that they planned to kill him while he was "stealing" the corn and so get rid of the evidence for the burials. José and Dinah planned an escape, but the military caught up with José in Bacolod, where he was thrown into prison and ended up in the cell next to me.

That was all behind them now. Their small house was their little haven. The breeze from the sea was pleasant, and baby and plants promised a new beginning. They had borrowed three thousand pesos from the Canadian Relief Fund for their charcoal-selling and had already paid back most of it.

Before I left, Dinah said to me, "There are people trying to put us off this land, Padre. Some have accepted a few pesos and gone, but the people in our row of houses have not moved. We refused because we know that this land is disputed land and they must first have a court order."

"That's true," I said.

"I have met with some of the others, and we have agreed to stick together."

"Then why don't you contact the priests in the cathedral and start a small Christian Community like the one you used to have in Hinoba-an?" I suggested. Then I said goodbye and promised to get in touch as soon as I had found a house to rent.

Search for a House

Ever since I came back I had been on the lookout for a house to rent in Bacolod. It would have to be big enough to house the offices of our magazine, *Misyon*, of which I was to be the editor. I hoped too that in some small way it might become a center for peace-building. But I was having a hard time. Some owners were unusually hostile. They could not have believed the accusation that we had killed Mayor Sola, the basis on which we had been jailed some years before. It had to be that they resented the Church's stand on land reform, which now threatened to become a reality since it had recently been incorporated into the new constitution. The next step would be a law passed by congress to implement that constitutional clause. A bitter battle was now going on in the restored congress as the Negros sugar plantation owners attempted to water down that law to nothing. The bishops had produced a series of television advertisements in favor of a stronger law. I had been featured in one of the clips, so that may have hindered me in my search.

I asked my old friend Lilly to help me. We met for lunch at a Chinese restaurant in Araneta Street.

I had first met Lilly some years before. A friend of mine, Putot, had been the truck driver on a small cooperative farm we had started in the mountains. The idea was that these cooperatives would plant sugar and other crops, which would all be worked and owned by the laborers themselves. Such was the dream: a crude attempt at an alternative to the sugar plantations, which cover 90 percent of the best land of Negros.

But tragedy hit Putot's life. He came home one day to find his wife Nena with another man. It was the children, in their innocence, who had alerted him. Putot hit Nena, and Nena packed her things and walked out, leaving him with the three children. Putot decided to leave the cooperative. I tried to help him look for Nena, but she went up to the city and found work among the clubs. I could not find her. After a few years Lilly appeared. She had a child of her own, but she took care of

Putot's three with great love and affection. After some time, when things were going well with them, Putot approached me and asked if I would bless their union? I promised to see what I could do, but it was just at that time that the military took the case of multiple murder against me and my friends. Soon after I was imprisoned, so I couldn't follow up Putot and Lilly's case.

It must have been a year or so later that Putot, being a good driver, was asked to drive a truck taking a crowd to a protest rally on the anniversary of Marcos's declaration of martial law. Putot had never been one to get politically involved, but he agreed to drive, and as the trucks, packed with standing peasants, lined up in the village of Tapi ready to leave, the military arrived. They examined the trucks and asked the various drivers to step down and, apparently at random, took Putot away. Lilly and the children never saw him again. Lilly spent the next two years going from military camp to military camp, searching for Putot. She got one fantastic story after another. The truth, she now knew, was that he had been killed and was buried in the military headquarters in the village of Tabo, but no one dared to go in and dig up the grave, even now that Marcos was gone. Lilly had changed from being a housewife to being head of a militant group of women called MARTYR: widows and orphans who banded together to help one another to survive and to search for their lost ones.

Lilly arrived at the restaurant with her four children. It did not turn out to be a very happy meal; Lilly had too many sad stories to tell me.

First, there was Noel, the youngest, eight years of age. He had been more deeply and visibly affected by the disappearance of his father than the others. At nighttime he would pray that the military would drop him into the river from the bridge, if they would only give back his *Tatay* ("father"). He even wrote to me (I was then studying in Maryknoll), asking me to pray to the infant Jesus for the return of his father. He paid no attention in class and drew guns on his copybook and kept going up to the other students and saying, "Bang, bang! You're dead." When Lilly remonstrated with him he said school was of no use with Tatay gone. When he grew up he planned to become a soldier and kill those who killed his father.

Susan, who was now thirteen, had become as hard as nails; that seemed to be her way of coping with the loss of first her mother and then her father, but Joel, her younger brother, now ten, had become silent. There was more. Nena, their real mother, had briefly reappeared and contrived to meet the children—possibly out of curiosity. "I am your mother," she said. Only Susan recognized her, and she responded, "You're not our mother. Our mother is at home."

The meal had been heavy going, not the joyful reunion I had expected. Several times I could hardly keep back my tears and I left feeling depressed.

I set off on the almost forty-mile drive south along the coast to our Columban headquarters in Himamaylan. That journey gives you a good idea of the island of Negros. Almost all the way the road is lined with sugar cane; it stretches to the mountains on the left side of the road and to the sea on the right. As I drove, scenes from our conversation kept returning, especially the image of Joel, the quiet one, begging his mother Nena not to leave them and then, when she continued to pack, begging her to take him with her. He had felt his mother's leaving more than the others, maybe because it was he who had told his father that there was another man in the house.

Of course I should never have driven straight after a midday meal in the tropical heat with so much on my mind. Unconsciously, my foot became heavier and heavier on the accelerator, especially when I got to that long stretch of uninterrupted road leading to the seawall at Valladolid. Suddenly I awoke from my thoughts about Joel and his mother to find the car moving at a terrible speed and veering off the road. A hundred yards ahead the seawall curved toward me. I must have been going very fast indeed because, though I locked the wheel fully to the left, the car hurtled on to the right toward the wall. The car hit the wall sideways. It should have toppled over into the sea, because the wall is so low, only a couple of feet high, but instead it banged along the wall for twenty yards and then suddenly, belatedly, the turned wheel began to take effect and the car swooped back to the road. It did a complete U-turn and then tore along in front of a row of little houses. When stopped, I was facing exactly in the direction from which I had come. Mercifully there was no traffic and not a soul on the road!

That evening, over a drink at headquarters by the sea at Himamaylan, our superior, Mickey Martin, said to me, "Niall, you'll be wanting someone to help you in your house, if you ever get it. I suggest you get someone who can help you with the driving when you're tired. You've so many long journeys to do. There's a young man in the local parish who has been clerk of the church for many years. He is earnest and reliable, but his father joined the New Peoples Army after their land was taken by a wealthy man in Bacolod City. The father has been killed. The boy has taken the death of his father very badly. His mother and the priests of the parish are afraid he will be drawn into the whole thing. It would be better for him to be out of harm's way in Bacolod, and he's a good cook too." That was my first introduction to Nonoi.

The next day I met Nonoi, a diminutive, wiry young man who looked straight at you with shining eyes. He was twenty-four, but for some reason he looked fifteen. Maybe it was his size and the ingenuous grin. While working with the priests, he had trained as a barefoot doctor in the Christian Communities in the surrounding mountains. He could pull teeth, give injections, do acupuncture, insert intravenous needles and make syrups and tinctures from local herbs; and he knew the workings of the Christian Communities. His work with the Communities had given him a passion for justice, as had the experience of losing the family land. He was willing to start as soon as he had talked it over with his widowed mother. She would be glad that he was moving out of the district. He could not drive, but he did have a student's license and I agreed to teach him. All I needed now was to go back to Bacolod to see if Lilly had had any luck finding a house to rent.

But before I went back to Bacolod I had a very important task — to make a painful visit to the sugar plantation where I had once lived.

Nanding

As I walked along the abandoned railway track into the plantation, memories began to come back to me. A long time ago, or it seemed like that to me now, when I was a young priest, I came to live on this plantation. It was by a sort of accident. The owner of the plantation, a good man, had donated land for a retreat house on his plantation. I became chaplain to the retreat house and built myself a comfortable native house nearby. Before I knew it, I was being drawn into the life of the plantation. Of the many events which took place on that hacienda while I was there one in particular is burned into my memory. I have written about it elsewhere but I retell it here with little change. When you read it I think you will understand why.

One night, shortly before Christmas, a knock came on my door. I opened the door. It was a young man, a laborer on the plantation. His name was Nanding, the pet name for Fernando. His wife, Clarita, was not well and was due to give birth. Would I bring her in my Volkswagen to the nearby sugar mill, which had a small hospital? The town itself, though very large, had no hospital and no ambulance. Nanding and his brother — and his father and his mother and Clarita's family too — worked on the hacienda, yet they had not gone to the administrator to borrow the hacienda pick-up. Maybe this was because not so long before Inting, the tractor driver, had been seriously sick but had been refused the loan of the hacienda transportation. The time lost seeking the administrator's help had proved fatal. Inting had died in my car. I lent Nanding the Volkswagen.

Next day Clarita gave birth to two very tiny baby girls. They were premature so, following the local custom, I baptized them right there in the hospital, Benilda and Margarita. The hospital had no incubator. They had made a makeshift one, using a light bulb as a heater; the babies took turns at the oxygen. Nanding had bought a tin of ordinary household milk for the babies.

The next day I sent over some special baby food and at night I visited them again, only to find that little Margarita had died.

The milk and the baby food were untouched. Benilda was alone in the "box with the bulb" and had the oxygen to herself. When I came back again Benilda was dead too. Nanding and Clarita could not even cry. They stared blankly.

That night I went for the first time to Nanding's house at the edge of a large sugar cane field. The thatched nipa-palm roof and the matting walls were so full of holes as to be almost useless against heavy rain or wind. When I went inside, I saw Margarita and Benilda laid out in dainty pink dresses on top of a wooden box. When I came nearer I realized that they were not really wearing dresses; it was crepe paper. I prayed for a short while and then sat on the floor with Nanding. There was no table or chair. He broke the silence.

"Padre, some say we should bury them in one coffin and some say two. What do you say, Padre?"

"What do you think yourself?"

"I think they should be buried in two coffins and in two graves, because they are two."

Nanding stayed up and watched the dead babies all that night. The next day they were buried in separate graves in the paupers' part of the town graveyard.

Two nights later I went to the hospital to visit Clarita. It was about 11 P.M. I was sitting by the bed and took Clarita's hand. She held my hand very tightly and said:

"Father, it is very painful. Don't go away."

The intravenous fluid had stopped flowing, so I looked for the nurse and then I looked for the doctor and asked him to examine Clarita. He did and wrote out a prescription and gave it to Nanding, who hurried off.

"Where's he going?" I asked. "Don't we have medicine in the hospital?"

"No," the nurse said. "If we kept medicine here, we'd never be paid for it. He has to go back to the hacienda to get the administrator to approve it. Then he can take it to the drugstore and wake them up and get the medicine."

"But that will take two hours!" I ran after Nanding and signed my name on the prescription clearly and sent a messenger over to the drugstore to get the medicine.

The medicine did not ease Clarita's pain at once. Nanding and I sat on the bed, each holding one of her hands.

"Father, if I die, please give advice to Nanding whenever he needs it." Nanding bent over Clarita, his tears dropping onto her face.

"Don't worry, Nanding. I won't die."

Finally the medicine reduced the pain, so I slipped away because I had a Mass at 4 A.M. for the Christmas novena. At 1 A.M. Clarita took off her wedding ring and asked Nanding to wear it. Around 2 A.M. she died.

After Mass I hurried back. I saw the faces and for the first time in my adult life I cried. Bitterly, openly.

The nine-day vigil after burial was held in Clarita's father's house because, though poor, it was a lot better than Nanding's own house. Everyone sat on the floor. The married women played Panginggi, a card game, using old Spanish-style cards. The girls and boys played Bordon, a sort of truth-or-consequences game. In the midst of the noise and laughter, Nanding lay on the floor, face down, exhausted, unconscious to the world.

Everyone, except me, was in rags. These were the laborers on a 220-acre sugar plantation that had earned over seventy-six thousand dollars the previous milling year — a great amount of money in those days. Each of the fifty-two families employed there received a little over two hundred dollars each for the whole year. And this was not in the category of bad haciendas!

I asked Nanding why Clarita had not had a prenatal check-up; they were supposed to do that free in the town.

"Well, you see," he said, "she had no clothes to go to town in and she had no money for the fare. I owe a lot because of my baby who died last year. So the administrator deducts from my earnings gradually to pay that debt. And the rest they take for our rice ration debt, which built up during the off-season. So we had no money in our hand at all, except what Clarita earned by washing clothes for people in the town, and that's why she kept working till the last moment."

"And I suppose that's why her womb burst. How much do you owe now?"

"P1,400.00" ($213.50).

I reckoned that if he and his surviving child, Nenita, did not fall sick it would take him several years to pay off the debt. But he would have to make his working clothes from fertilizer sacks and keep to a bare rice and dried fish ration.

Nanding was deeply attached to Nenita. During the height of his troubles he had entrusted her to the care of his in-laws. After the funeral he came to me worried lest, having left her with them for a time, he had forfeited his rights to the child.

"Of course not," I said, although I was not too sure. "Does Nenita remember her mother?"

"Oh, yes! Because when anybody asks her 'Where's your mother?' she says, 'She's in the graveyard covered in sand.' "[1]

Though Nanding's story was one of many, I find myself coming back to it because it brought home to me the reality of the island. It is true that there are many beautiful exceptions. There are people in sugar who live personally impeccable lives. There are people in sugar who lead lives of intense Christian devotion. There are even some who have spent their life working to reform the system[2] but the overall reality is that the sugar industry with all its sub-systems works together to reduce the peasant population to a state of serfdom and penury that cries out to heaven.

When I went back to the plantation this time, I wanted to be able to report that things were changing for the better since Marcos had gone and Cory Aquino had come. Some of my fellow Columbans chided me for my optimism, even naiveté. This was my chance to prove them wrong.

On the way into the plantation I thought that the houses had improved slightly. Did I see some rice growing where sugar cane had been before? After an emotional reunion, I sat down with the women and men and asked them about their lives now. This farm was paying the minimum wage of P67 a day (about three dollars). The owner here had always paid the legal minimum, but the legal minimum wage always lagged behind inflation and was barely adequate to meet the day-to-day food needs of the family and not their clothing, education or medicine.[3] The most that could be said about the minimum wage was that it was the wage below which laborers would not have enough strength to work. Though right beside the town, the houses still did not have electricity, water or sanitation. The people washed at a well or in a river and used the fields as toilets.

How about the labor union? Yes, the labor union was now active; in my day it had been afraid to move. However, the leader told me that he had been called in by the chief of police in the town and ominously warned. He had answered that union members were not communists but were merely pushing to have the basic labor laws implemented. Yet the very fact that he had been called in by the police was a warning signal to the other laborers. It was still an uphill battle to get owners to grant such things as social security benefits and medicare. When the union asked to meet the owner, he responded by calling in the workers, one by one, and trying to frighten or buy them off. Some are always intimidated.

And how about the land reform program? Well, they knew nothing about it. That I could not understand. What about the sixty-thirty-ten, the governor's own land-reform program? The idea was that the owner would keep 60 percent of the land; 30 percent would be a joint cooperative; and 10 percent would go to the laborers. Well, this *hacendero* had not implemented the 30 percent joint cooperative, but he had given, *on loan*, a parcel to each laborer, amounting in all to 8 percent of the land. That helped a little; although it was utterly inadequate, it had the effect of letting the laborers farm for themselves. Maybe the memory of a long-lost self-reliance and independence would be touched. This could be a beginning. The problem was that, apart from the governor and a few others, no one was implementing the sixty-thirty-ten.[4] That was to be expected because, even by the government's own count, hardly 50 percent of the *hacenderos* were paying the minimum wage.[5] (The National Federation of Sugar Workers said it was as low as 3 percent.) Now the minimum wage was compulsory; the sixty-thirty-ten was voluntary.

Nanding was there with the others. He was happy to see me. He still worked in the fields, but he looked weak and aged beyond his years; he looked ten years older than myself, though he was ten years younger. He had never remarried.

"Where is Nenita?" I asked, recalling that she had come to visit me when I was in prison a few years before and I had arranged for her high school. No, she had not continued. I did not push Nanding for an explanation. Where was she now? In Manila, looking for work, but she had got sick. That was the news. Nanding smiled weakly at me as if to apologize.

I never got to know you, Nanding, in all those years. I pushed bright suggestions at you. You with three children dead; Nenita now gone; Clarita in the graveyard covered in sand.

In three of the houses I visited people were seriously sick. Two, in fact, were in danger of death and had no hope of adequate medical care. I visited my old friend Padut. She had five boys. The oldest, Tony, had been caught stealing scrap iron and had been killed by a security guard of the local sugar mill. Now two of her boys were in prison for killing a security guard in the same mill. (Revenge? I don't know.) Her only girl, Lila, had just returned from Manila, where she had worked in a big house as a maid. The son of her employer had made her pregnant. She had come home to have the child. We sat on the floor, tears streaming down the faces of Padut and Lila, as they told me the story.

"And do you know that after doing that to her," she said, "they want to take the child? We will never give it to them. This child is ours."

As I passed between the sugar cane fields on my way home, I knew why part of me had been reluctant to come. But the visit gave me a renewed clarity of understanding. The years away, the distance, coupled with the return and seeing things fresh again, had convinced me of two things. The first was that the problem in the sugar fields was not just the wages; it was the very way the whole sugar industry was and had always been organized. By having people working only six months a year and begging for hand-outs during the other six months, working this year to pay off last year's debts, the spirit in them was crushed.

The second thing I realized was consequent on this: Though working to raise the minimum wage is a laudable and a worthwhile struggle, and unionizing and working for social security and the basic human needs are necessary if people are to survive and grow, nevertheless Negros will never be a land of joy or peace till sugar is gone.[6]

The history of sugar has always been this way. Of the ten million people sold into slavery in the years when the slave ships plied the seas, some seven million were sold to the sugar fields. Sugar in those days was synonymous with slavery and slavery with sugar. American historian Robert Fogel writes in *Without Consent or Contract* that sugar planters led the way in the development of the new industrial/labor discipline:

> Slaves were organized into highly coordinated and precisely functioning gangs with no option but to work as ordered. They had no rights, they were treated as animals; punishment for idleness was severe and the workload was unrelentingly exhausting. Small wonder that white emigrants from the old world would have nothing to do with it, that the indigenous Indian people died out and that, as the plantations expanded, the cry from the colonies went out: "Send more slaves."[7]

But the Spaniards, to their credit, outlawed slavery very early in the Philippines. So Nicolas Loney and his friends — the mid-nineteenth-century parents of the Negros sugar industry — used debt-slavery as a substitute in order to hold the peasants in the fields.[8]

Technically their method is different; for Nanding it is the same.

Morit de los Santos

We finally managed to get a house beside the Bacolod abattoir or the slaughter house, as it was locally known. Nonoi moved in with me, and I started to put the office together.

It was sad to see the animals being herded past our house —

water buffaloes, cows, pigs and even spindly horses on their way
to be butchered. In recent months the refugees had been selling
their farm animals in order to buy food for their uprooted families. It was particularly disturbing to see the young water buffaloes. These were the mainstay of the small mountain farmer,
and for that reason, by law, they were supposed not to be butchered. Now they were on their way to the abattoir to be felled
by an axe and then attacked with knives. At night, as I lay in
bed, I would hear the last desperate screams of the pigs.

Noinoi found plenty to do, apart from helping me, because
evacuees were pouring into Bacolod from various parts of the
island and taking refuge at the seminary or protesting at the
Capitol Building, the governor's official office. The remote cause
of this wave of refugees was a little book called *The War of the
Flea*,[9] a manual on guerrilla warfare. One of the author's central
points was that the ultimate resource of the guerrilla is the people. While people were denied their basic human rights, they
would always be friendly to the guerrilla. When the people were
genuinely content, there was no place for the guerrilla; when
the people were miserable, they were the friendly water in which
the guerrilla swam. Any government that really wanted to end
a guerrilla war of this type had one thing to do: treat its people
properly. With the necessary reforms the guerrillas would have
nowhere to go, that is, nowhere to go spiritually; they would lose
their raison d'être. The water would have dried up.

Some Philippine military had been reading this book and
unfortunately missed the whole point. If the people were the
water in which the fish, the guerrillas, swam, then, they reckoned, if they took away the water, the fish would be left panting
on dry land. Solution: clear out the people from their homes in
the mountains where the New Peoples Army took refuge and
operated from and the NPA would be left helpless and foodless,
panting, as it were, on the dry lake bed. So, to clear the people
the military command in Negros ordered the shelling and bombing of the mountain areas. Thousands and thousands of people
fled the mountains, abandoning their belongings and carrying
with them their babies and their young children and pulling

along their farm animals.[10] And the New Peoples Army? Were they left panting on dry land? Not at all. These "fish" had feet. They ran away to another mountain. The military had read the metaphor too literally.

Meanwhile refugee centers all over the island were crammed. Hundreds of children were dying.[11] The priests of the diocese signed a "Collegial Statement" in protest. Some of the newspaper columnists were more shocked at the "Collegial Statement" than at the deaths of the children! Their attitude seemed to be that people are either "with us" or "against us" in this war; there's no middle ground. These so-called human rights activists, they felt, were lending solace to the enemy.[12]

When he was not helping me, Nonoi worked hard, bringing medicine and food to the evacuees. He also found time to help Dinah and José, the charcoal sellers, because Dinah had developed a very serious infection in her lower legs and feet, which was aggravated by the charcoal dust to which she was allergic. So chronic was the infection that the doctor said that if something was not done, she would face amputation of both feet. We got her into the Bacolod Sanitarium and after a few weeks she was able to go home to José and the child Andrea. But they needed to get their loan with the Canadian Relief Fund, which had loaned them money for their charcoal-selling business.

Then one day our phone rang. It was Dinah calling from a public phone. She was almost incoherent. But the gist of her message was that José had left the house for a few minutes the night before to relieve himself. He had not returned. In the morning she had heard an announcement on the radio that the dead body of a man had been found behind the Bacolod Sanitarium. The man had been shot to death. She had given Andrea to a neighbor to watch and gone to the sanitarium. It was José.

Dinah and her child and Nonoi and a few neighbors formed the congregation when I said the Requiem Mass for José there at their little house. Dinah took the lid off the coffin so that Andrea could have a last look at her father before we went to the grave. It was a pathetic little gathering, and of course there was also an air of fear. Some people felt that the fact that Dinah had been so vocal about not moving had something to do with José's abduction and death. (He must have been abducted when he went out of the house that night; a shot would have been too easily heard.) One of the unexplained details in his death was that the police announcement of the discovery of his body said that he wore a fatigue cap. That lined José with some subversive group or other and gave the impression that maybe he was a rebel caught red-handed. Dinah said that José had no such cap and, when she asked again and again to be shown the cap, the police were not able to produce it. It was difficult for her to keep going back because it was all she could do to support herself and Andrea. She could not push the cart because of her allergy to the charcoal dust, so she took up selling cigarettes at the street corner. She gave up going back to the police head-quarters, but she was more determined than ever not to move her shack.

Nonoi's own family had to evacuate from the mountains during the military campaign, which was activated all over the island. He built a house for them in the town of Binalbagan, and his young fiancée moved in with his mother and younger brothers and sisters. In the shelling of the mountains his cousin had been hit by shrapnel. Nonoi felt great anger. The children of many of his family's neighbors had died. He was becoming impatient, and we found ourselves arguing. I had invited the famous peace activists Jean and Hildegard Goss-Mayr to Baco-lod, and I suggested to Nonoi that he go along and hear Jean speaking on active nonviolence as a road to justice.

Jean and Hildegard arrived in Bacolod. Between them they had an extraordinary record of working for peace. In Algeria in the fifties they had helped to expose the massacres and atrocities of the French Army and had played a significant part in getting the French to withdraw from that country. They had spent much time in Warsaw and Prague, developing the nonviolent approach; they had worked all over Europe for the abolition of conscription and at the Vatican Council for the Church's blessing on conscientious objection. They had worked in Brazil on plantations not unlike Negros. They had known Ralph Abernathy, Helder Camara and Oscar Romero. Their central message was the linking of work for justice and work for peace; one could not advance without the other.

Attending the seminar was a group from the parish of Himamaylan, companions of Nonoi when he was working with the Christian Communities there. In the middle of the seminar some terrible news arrived. During the night several Scout Rangers from the military detachment in Carabolan, Himamaylan, had gone to the house of Morit de los Santos, the head of the justice and peace committee of the parish of Himamaylan and the right-hand man of the Sisters in their social work. He was also president of the Basic Christian Communities. The Scout Rangers had surrounded the house and attacked it with high-powered rifles and grenade launchers.

They had killed Morit and his wife and three of their children; a fourth, Joaquin, had survived by playing dead. Then the soldiers had gone up into the house and taken Joaquin's new basketball shoes, a radio and other personal belongings. They left, taking with them Morit's famous fighting cocks.

Since Morit was known to everyone, it was a terrible shock to the seminar, especially as Jean and Hildegard were dealing with this very topic. The participants from Himamaylan, headed by Sister Brigid, an Irish Presentation Sister, decided to leave the seminar and go home to see how they could help. Nonoi and myself drove the 40 miles south to the house, a little bit outside the town of Himamaylan. There were huge holes in the walls from the grenade launchers; blood was spilt everywhere. Over at the Convento, the parish house, the parish priest, Father Eamonn Gill, told us how he had gone straightway after the shooting and anointed the dead family. He had taken photographs; they were terrible to look at. A ten-year-old surviving child, who had spent the night with relatives, arrived on the scene when Father Gill was taking the photos. With extraordinary calmness she asked him to photograph her kissing her dead mother and father goodbye before they were removed to be placed in the coffins. Eamonn could not hold back his tears. "In all my years since I became a man, I have never been so moved."

In fact, he and Fr. Tom Marti, the Maryknoller who gave me this account, managed later to gain an audience with President Aquino and actually confronted her with the photographs. She suggested that there could have been NPA rebels in the house. "Then where were their bodies? I went there straight after the shooting," Eamonn Gill said. She suggested that they had taken the bodies away. The suggestion was too banal to answer because the Scout Rangers were completely surrounding the house. Anyway, Eamonn knew the full story from Joaquin, the young boy who had played dead. Tom felt that General Fidel Ramos, then Army Chief of Staff, and General de Villa, standing by the president's side, had given her these answers beforehand. Morit had worked for the government; if they suspected him of being a rebel, they only had to arrest him.

President Aquino had been visibly shaken when the photos of the bullet-torn children were passed to her. Nevertheless, she concluded the meeting by reminding all present that foreigners should not get involved in these cases.[13]

Fr. Gill himself refused to make any public comment on the meeting, because he said he had given that guarantee beforehand. All he would say was that "she is a woman without compassion."

The real reason for the massacre was clear to all of us. The parish of Himamaylan had been involved for many years in building small Christian Communities and in actively protesting serious human rights abuses. The Presentation Sisters ran many community projects for the poor. This was at a time when the rebels or New Peoples Army had overrun some of the third-rate farmland in the foothills outside the town of Himamaylan. The heavy military presence and action of the Philippine Armed Forces meant that some of this land was beginning to be taken back from the rebels. These government officials saw any criticism of the army and the attention paid to the peasants in the foothills by the Church as friendship with the enemy.[14] The killing of Morit and later of other Himamaylan parish leaders was a warning to all to stop cooperating with the Church's program.

Nonoi, who knew Morit intimately because he had worked

with him, was badly shaken. There had been messages broadcast on the radio threatening Morit and others working with the Church, but he had taken them in his stride. This massacre showed just how far the military was prepared to go. I suggested to Nonoi that maybe the time had come to increase his medical skills. It was obvious how useful he was during the height of the evacuees' crisis. It was possible for him to do a course in para-medics on another island.

Nonoi agreed to go, but we had many straight conversations before he left. He showed me the utmost respect: I was a priest; I was older; I was also his employer. He respected each of these three things deeply. But he quietly repeated his conviction that, though he was content to work as a paramedic and help people in that way, nevertheless he was personally convinced that the situation in Negros, even now that Marcos was gone and democ-racy, such as it was, was restored, warranted the use of arms. Though he did not have the terminology, he was presenting me with the age-old just-war theory, present in every moral theology textbook since St. Augustine.

Nonoi had never heard of the just-war theory. He did not even know the history of Negros — few people did. It was not taught in the schools. If he did, he might have been even more sure of himself. It is necessary now to take a brief look at that history if we are to understand fully what is happening in Negros. Our present is the child of the past.

Magellan and Lapu-Lapu

Ferdinand Magellan, the Portuguese explorer working for the Spanish Crown, stumbled on the Philippines in 1521. In fact, he was killed on the Island of Mactan by the warrior Lapu-Lapu, not too far south of the Island of Negros. The Victoria, the last remaining ship of his fleet of five, limped home across the Indian Ocean and in September 1522 staggered into San Lucar, the port of Cadiz — the first to circumnavigate the globe.

Though Magellan's invasion failed, the Spaniards returned

and occupied and colonized the Philippines till they were ousted by the Americans in 1898.

The islands were a medley of diverse and ancient cultures, which carried on trade with places as far away as North Vietnam. Religion and laws flourished alongside such activities as boatbuilding, pottery, weaving and the working of silver and gold. Though agriculture was only at a subsistence level it provided adequately and even abundantly. Early Spaniards noted that the inhabitants of Panay, the island neighboring Negros, were able to read and write using their own syllabary. The first Spaniards told of the gentleness and generosity with which they were greeted.

The Spaniards introduced Christianity and much of Spanish culture. But somehow they never really got to Negros in the same way as they got to the other islands, partly due to lack of men, but also due to the Moro or Muslim pirates, who continually wiped out the Christian outposts on Negros.

So Negros dreamed on with its tribal religion and laws and culture and self-reliance largely intact.[15] Then four things happened all at once in the mid-nineteenth century:

—The Suez Canal was opened; more Spaniards were on the way.

—The steamship came into common use; the Moro pirates found themselves outclassed.

—America and England forced Spain to open Iloilo, a port on the neighboring island of Panay, to trade.

—Nicolas Loney, an adventurous British entrepreneur, arrived with the title of Honorary British Consul to the Island of Panay.

Nicolas Loney got to work immediately. In Panay he found a thriving textile industry. Handwoven textiles of great beauty were supplied to the rest of the islands and exported to various parts of the world. Thirteen thousand looms operated in the town of Jaro alone. Loney pirated the patterns and sent them to Manchester, where using steam-driven looms and cheap slave cotton from the United States he reproduced them at a much lower cost. He then imported these to Iloilo and within a few short years had captured the market and its outlets. The looms of Panay fell silent. Loney was now a rich man, but not rich enough. He worried that his ships were returning to England empty. It was then he hit on sugar.[16]

Ever since the thirteenth century, Europe had been addicted to sugar. To support this addiction Europeans rediscovered slavery and set up the tropical plantations of Latin America and the West Indies. Now, Loney would produce sugar as cheap as these plantations, and he would do it on the island of Negros.

He imported machinery from Britain and set up a sugar plantation in Talisay north of Bacolod. Then he set about organizing bank loans for the Chinese entrepreneurs from Iloilo, many of whom he had just driven out of the textile industry; this was their consolation prize. Soon a great invasion of Negros was underway, with Loney advancing the capital for the new sugar farms.

Getting the land from the native peoples posed a problem. After all, some of them had been there for a thousand years, and the Spanish laws actually favored the native holders. Apart from lobbying to change these laws, Loney and his friends had many ways of getting the land; sometimes they used legal ploys, in other cases straightforward massacre.[17] Some future generation of Negrenses will unearth those files somewhere in Madrid and weep before the truth.

Through the next hundred years, although momentarily stalled by several peasant revolts and World War II, sugar marched along the rich western alluvial plain, then round the heel of the island, then into the uplands and finally into the hidden mountain valleys, seeking out the last of the ancient tribal peoples who had not submitted, reducing them to laborers on the land they once tilled. Today sugar rears its head over nearly 744,000 acres with all the bitter consequences that that brings.[18]

A traveler now would see a far different sight than met the eyes of those first Spanish adventurers. From north to south a sea of waving sugar stretches for almost 125 miles, sporadically broken by a few remaining spots of rice and increasingly interrupted by the walls of guarded prawn farms. Negros does not feed herself now.[19] The great rain forests of mahogany and teak are gone; the mountains are bare. Most of the rivers are dry gulches for half the year and dangerous torrents for the rest of the year, carrying away life and livestock and precious soil to the sea;[20] this river-borne soil settles over the coral spawning grounds of the fish, smothering their eggs at birth.[21] The mangroves, favorite nesting place of the fish, surrender to great mechanical diggers preparing the ground for prawns for export to Japan.[22] No birds sing, for the tree-based birds are gone. So are the deer and wild pigs and the flocks of graceful Tulabong, which used to perch on the backs of the water buffaloes. In places even the coconut trees face the chain saw.

And the people . . . where are they? Negros has many cities and towns, some handsome and prosperous, but most of Negros is still plantations. With certain praiseworthy exceptions, a great number of the plantation houses are shacks bereft of furniture. People sleep in rows upon the floor and frequently the moon looks in through gaping holes in roof and walls — and people huddle in corners when it rains. Daytime brings the fields and the drudgery of backbreaking work in the tropical sun without adequate food or clothing. Much worse than that is the seasonal layoff period where workers queue for handouts to be paid out of the wages of the coming year. It is that enforced idleness and mind-sapping dependence which is the real evil of the cane field. There, for many, life is worse than death; it is a sort of half life that gauntly stares from ten thousand paneless windows — lethargic, listless, cowed, suppliant, devoid of hope. Children line up at soup kitchens with outstretched rice bowls. "Please, ma'am, may I have some more?"

The schools that serve these children are run down: no lights to study by, no books, a page to write on bought for five centavos before the class begins.

Hospitals are overcrowded, with patients sometimes lying along the corridors. A rat peeps from beneath a bed. Yet these are the lucky ones. Most die without any professional medical attention at all; they are carried off in makeshift coffins to graves unmarked, save for some paper flowers placed with love. Many have fled or wandered to the city where they live in cardboard huts put together from cartons and old election signboards, promising prosperity.

For me, the great enigma is that so many Christians sincerely concerned about the people do not realize the depth of their suffering. And those who do find it difficult, if not impossible, to communicate it to others. Sometimes in Manila we would meet dear friends who had land interests in Negros. They would briefly ask how things were in Negros. "How is the peace and order situation?" was frequently the way they phrased it. But the topic was whisked away to something more lighthearted immediately.

How does one lift the veil on reality? I believe that sometimes it is the little thing that does it. At least this is so for me.

—The dead batteries put out in the sun in the hope of bringing back a little life.

—The little boy ashamed to go out because he has to wear his sister's dress while his only pair of pants is being washed.

—A whole village wearing secondhand clothes from Manila.

—A mother beside me at the drugstore who orders a *minudo* of cough syrup for her child and watches the attendant drain half the cough syrup from an already small bottle.

—A man cleaning his teeth with sand.

—Hungry people boiling river stones to make a sort of soup.

—A woman plowing a field at 4 A.M.

—A wife, weak with tuberculosis, sleeping all night with her head on her husband's outstretched arm; they have no pillow.

—A widow making porridge from rice husks for her hungry children.

These little things gave me a glimpse behind that veil. But how do we get inside the feelings of these people? Let me recall two occasions when for a moment the chord which sounded in their hearts seemed also to vibrate in mine.

I had been called to baptize a sick baby on a wealthy sugar plantation. The child was far gone; his eyes were rolling back, revealing the whites. I asked the distressed mother if we could bring the child to the hospital. Reluctantly she agreed, but first said she must clothe him.

She went to a cardboard carton in the corner of the shack to look for a cloth in which to wrap the child. She rummaged in the box, rejecting the first two cloths as being too ragged. She delved further, pulling out more rags. As she neared the bottom of the box, with still no respectable cloth to wrap her child in, a terrible look of panic filled her face. I can never forget that look.

Another moment like that I have recorded elsewhere:

I had not been on the plantation a week before I knew it was a completely different reality from what I had known before. The people were thin, sickly, and in rags. Most nights coming home I would see lights burning in one of the houses. It was usually a wake. There were always wakes ... so rarely for the old. One night my Volks was waved down by Tia Carmen, a widow and herb healer. She asked me to drive a young couple home. They got silently into the back, carrying a white bundle — their dead child. They had not been able to afford the hospital, and Tia Carmen had done what she could. We drove in silence toward the plantation where they lived with their grandparents, about ten miles away near the sea. I drove the Volks right under their house, which was on stilts. They got out and went up. At first I remained below, but then I followed them up. No one noticed me as I stood in the shadow of the outside awning. The young couple broke down when they saw their grandparents. The faces of the old people crinkled up as if to cry, but no tears came — only spasms of pain and distress. The grandmother took the little bundle in her arms, and looking in at the face, addressed the dead child: "Inday, little one, we went into debt just to keep you alive." The desolation was overpowering. I backed away and went quietly down the stairs. I have never forgotten that night.[23]

Another time occurred while I was writing this book. Early one morning, as I was dressing and casually looking out of my window onto the street in the city of Bacolod, I saw an oldish woman walking by, carrying a large mound of watercress upon her head. Suddenly she collapsed, falling straight to the ground. A young man abandoned his bicycle and lifted her to the side of the road. Pulling on the rest of my clothes I hurried down and out the gate.

"She has fainted from weakness," the young man said. We cradled her and she began to speak, as if to someone who was not there.

"Don't worry, I'll get food. Your mother will soon be better and your father will be given back his job. I'll get food."

We brought her to the yard in front of my house and put her on an iron garden chair. She went on talking, semicoherently. I brought her some rice; she couldn't swallow it.

Someone said, "She hasn't eaten for three days. The only thing she'll be able to take is bread dipped in a little milk."

I got bread, which I dipped in a little tinned milk heated with hot water. She could swallow that and, as she recovered, she told us that she had walked all the way into the city from a sugar plantation on the outskirts in the hope of selling the watercress. Her daughter was sick and the family had not eaten for two days. She had not eaten for three. Her son-in-law had lost his job on the plantation because he had joined a labor union. We bought her bundle and she insisted on going home.

Though one could point to landowners who have struggled for years to try and change things, sometimes with extraordinary perseverance, nevertheless things are *not* changing. Negros is in the grip of sugar like some mysterious deadly weed or fatal addiction. Independent social observers[24] will agree that Nicolas Loney's creation has become a monster. It now has a life of its own, producing thousands upon thousands of hungry children, often mentally damaged, who as adults will never find a way out of this hungry land, except perhaps to stumble into the over-crowded slums at the edge of a city or maybe make their way to the brothels of Manila. All this for sugar, an unnecessary and even harmful addiction, which the human race does not need.[25]

The present conditions in Negros are part of a long development, going back more than a hundred years. During that time the peasants have moved steadily from a life of frugality to a life of penury, and from a life of penury to a life of destitution. Now, as we turn the century, their inner spirit is being corroded by the recurring need for soup kitchens and handouts. For the sugar workers Negros is gradually becoming a great concentration camp kept in line by various branches of the armed forces.[26] These forces put ever greater weight on the lid of the boiling pot, but never help to lower the flame beneath it. With their forced evacuations they make a desert of the uplands, and they call it peace. Shades of Tacitus!

Nothing but drastic *structural* changes can turn things around. Nothing has happened in all this time to suggest that those who hold power are prepared to make these changes voluntarily. The opportunity for a new start and a genuine land reform following the 1986 people's power revolution, which brought Cory Aquino to power, has been missed. There are many brave and principled exceptions, but landlords as a class have used their power and influence and money and sometimes guns to rob the Comprehensive Land Reform Law of its effectiveness.[27] Most haciendas go on as before. The peasants of Negros are grievously oppressed, and oppression is built into the social, economic and political system. They suffer daily the violence of this system, the violence defined by Archbishop Oscar Romero as "institutional violence." The battle between Lapu-Lapu and Magellan still goes on.

While some Christians agonize over what their social and political response should be to the long-standing institutionalized violence of the Island of Negros, others, with strong support from different sources, argue that social and political involvement is far from what Christ intended for Christians and indeed leads to spiritual destruction; Christians should stay out of it. This opinion is passionately held and widely propagated.

Thus the Christians of Negros are divided by this social question as sharply as the island itself is divided by its jagged, volcanic Cordillera.

So where does the Church stand?

PART II

RESPONDING TO VIOLENCE

To Be Neither Victims Nor Oppressors

[2]

Where Does the Church Stand?

A Bomb for Fortich

A little after midnight on Tuesday, April 28, 1987, a jeep slowed down along Lacson Street in the City of Bacolod just beside the old priests' home where Bishop Antonio Fortich had taken refuge after his house was burned by the Marcos military.[1] The jeep halted, but the engine kept running; out jumped a figure. He paused for a moment to get his bearings, then carefully lobbed an object over the outside wall into the courtyard toward the bishop's room. Then he ran back to the jeep and sped away.

The object was sailing straight for the alcove at the door of the bishop's bedroom. Almost at the end of its flight it hit the branch of a tree in the patio and fell five yards short of its intended destination, landing on the earth of the patio. It exploded with a great blast, flinging steel fragments in every direction, smashing the louvers of the bishop's chapel; taking cement off the walls all around and piercing the door of the bishop's office. A few yards further would have increased the impact; it would certainly have reached the sleeping bishop himself. As it was, despite the absorbing effect of the earth, the grenade took chunks off a wall ten yards away. The only casualty was a little sparrow.

Was the bomb intended to kill the bishop? Or was that bomb

33

intended to kill the vision that the bishop had come to stand for? To be a disciple of Jesus in Negros today means setting one's face against injustice and working for social change.

The more immediate question for us, however, is this: Can the idea that being a Christian involves setting one's face against injustice stand up before the court of Christian wisdom and tradition?

The people who threw the bomb sent a cassette tape with a message on it to the local radio station in Bacolod. They claimed responsibility and said they were the Kristianos Kontra Komunismo.

For them Monsignor Fortich's call for a cease-fire, for just wages, for land reform, was the thin end of the wedge of communism. They represent the extreme end of the spectrum of those who question the Church's involvement in justice issues. But there are others, not so obviously violent, who give the support and comfort necessary for the extremes to exist.

A devout Negros family in a southern town had been involved in promoting religion for years. It was the time of great evacuations in the south of Negros caused by the Philippine military shelling the mountains. Hundreds of children died in the exercise and thousands of people were reduced to misery. During my two-hour visit to that landed family our discussion ranged to Fatima, the blue army of our Lady, the need for the pope to consecrate Russia to the Virgin Mary—I protested that he had already done this but they explained he had not done so *in unison* with the bishops.[2] Then we moved to Medjugorje, and rosaries turning into gold, and on and on through various marvels with never a word about the war, about the refugees, about the dying children. I knew that this was not a welcome subject. I did not bring it up; I knew that for them it would be considered a distraction from the quest for holiness. For them, religion was complete without involvement in such secular matters.

This view may seem preposterous in the light of the Church's unambiguous teaching on justice in the Second Vatican Council, but when I came to Negros that view was the common one. It was held by most of the faithful, most of the priests and especially the old and saintly bishop Emmanuel Yap. Indeed, looking back, my own view was not too far from that either.

This view separated radically religion and life, particularly social life. Two anecdotes from the time of Bishop Yap illustrate how wide the chasm was.

In 1964, the year I arrived in Negros, I was for a brief few days acting parish priest of the large and handsome southern town of Kabankalan. Bishop Yap was due on his pastoral visit, a rare and important occasion. He was to be met by me outside the town. He would then walk in procession under a canopy to the church preceded by a band and followed by the people. As he passed the town hall the popular mayor, Vicente Garcia, would put a lei around his neck. I conceived of the plan of getting the bishop at that moment to step inside the town hall — only a matter of yards away — to see the prisoners. I suppose I was anxious for a gesture of concern for the poor; the prisoners were a wretched bunch, twenty squashed into a cell that should fit two. Sardines lived a charmed life compared with these prisoners. Getting the bishop to detour into the prison, I admit now, was a form of hijack, but he did consent. The gate was swung open and those ragged men fell on their knees before the bishop, whom I asked to give them a blessing, which he did. Then, keeping them on their knees, he proceeded to give them a harsh lecture on repentance and reform. Even at that early stage I realized that these prisoners were in for mostly trifling crimes or even on false charges, and that being in prison did not mean they were guilty. That image of the corpulent old bishop in purple socks, purple belly band and purple skull cap wagging his forefinger in reproach at the almost prostrate prisoners spoke to me painfully of the chasm between the religion I represented and the life of the people.

The old bishop was a devout and a frugal man, loved by his priests. I'm sure he'll forgive me recalling just one more story. It illustrates not so much him as his time.

It is the Fiesta Mass in the inland town of Payao. The bishop has chosen to speak in English, though the congregation is poor and Ilonggo-speaking. He has chosen to speak on the Friday law of abstinence from meat, though the daily fare of this congregation is fish and the abstinence law does not bind in the Philippines (a privilege to the Spanish Crown). He reminds the congregation that some whales have been washed up recently on the northern coast of Negros (a freak event, whales are unknown in these seas). He explains that the whale, contrary to some opinions, is not a fish. It is an animal, and therefore its flesh is meat. The proof: it suckles its young. It is a mammal, and then the triumphant conclusion: you *cannot* eat whale on a Friday. Silence. He turns to Fr. Tom Revatto, the Irish parish priest, and asks him to translate.

At that very moment, Bishop Yap's brother bishops in Rome at the Second Vatican Council were writing: "The joys and hopes, the griefs and anguish of men and women of our time, especially those who are poor and afflicted in any way, are the joys and hopes, the griefs and anguish of the followers of Christ as well."

Bishop Yap did not attend the Vatican Council but he did send a written intervention—a request that the rite of infant baptism not be changed. When the ordinance came from the Council asking for altars to be changed and the Mass to be said facing the people, he refused point blank and said, in effect, only over his dead body. Many other bishops and priests preferred not to turn around toward the people. Their refusal was powerfully symbolic because everything that the Council was trying to do could be symbolized in that one action of turning toward the people, closing the gap between religion and life.

Though I was all for the Council, I did not for quite some time understand the implication of closing the gap between religion and life. For example, I used to bring communion around to the sick. There were so many on our list that the visits became at times perfunctory. I recall I used to visit one little boy in a wretched shack which reeked of urine, naturally, because the little fellow couldn't move from his bed. I don't remember any parents being around. Maybe he was twelve years of age, thin and spindly, lying on his bed. His eyes shone so brightly with joy at my coming that even thirty years later in my memory they are not dimmed. He received communion each time devoutly, and I am sure I took time to pray with him, but I am certain I never asked what was wrong or whether I could help cure it. Of course I had no money, but that was not the point. I was on a spiritual visit; the material side of things was not my concern. I returned faithfully every Tuesday till that day I found him gone. I would do many things differently today.

Then Bishop Yap died. It was October 16, 1966. For the funeral at the Cathedral of San Sebastian, Fortich, then the vicar capitular — the man who runs the diocese while it waits word from Rome on who the new bishop will be — erected a temporary altar and said the first Mass facing the people.

A New Type of Bishop

We knew that it would be against normal policy for Fortich to be appointed as bishop in his own diocese. But through the Cursillo retreat movement, which he organized, Fortich had won the hearts of the powerful *hacenderos*. Most of them owed their return to the Church to him. That influential lobby let it be known to the papal nuncio that they wanted Fortich as bishop of Bacolod. So, when the news broke on 16 January 1967 of his appointment to Bacolod, the wealthy of Negros were overjoyed. They presented the bishop-elect with a new black Mercedes Benz. It was air-conditioned and had patrician-looking white covers fitted to the seats. Bottles of twelve-year-old Johnny Walker and Chivas Regal were stacked up in the bishop's house.

The nuncio may have appointed Fortich in part due to pressure from the *hacenderos*, but he himself was a man who had caught the spirit of the Second Vatican Council and with the appointment he gave Fortich a special message. This was just a few months after the appearance of the encyclical letter *Populorum Progressio* — the most progressive Church document since Leo XIII's *Rerum Novarum* in 1891. At his episcopal ordination on 24 February 1967, the nuncio took Fortich aside and said: "The Holy Father appointed you bishop of Bacolod so that you will do something for the poor." Most of the real poor at this stage did not even know that there was a bishop in Bacolod or a pope in Rome. By the same token, many of the rich were hardly any more aware of the existence of the poor; to them they were a vague mass known collectively as "these people," but rarely recognized as individual, feeling persons.

Historians, social scientists and journalists are always asking what prompted Fortich to launch his social programs. The first concrete push came from a now forgotten event — the Rural Congress. The congress was initiated by and orchestrated from Rome as part of the practical attempt to implement *Populorum Progressio*. Ironically, a social movement that was to foster the idea of change from below got its first stimulus from above.

The Rural Congress was held in Bacolod in September 1967, six months after Bishop Fortich was installed as third bishop of Bacolod. A prelate from Rome attended; Cardinal Santos gave it his backing and sent Bishop Gaviola to represent him. For the first time in Negros, a group of high level Church people tried to understand a little of what the poor were suffering and to make plans to do something about it. Fortich listened carefully. The congress came up with resolutions outlining steps to be taken by the Church toward radical social reform. The mood after the congress was euphoric and looking back at it years later Fortich said that it was one of the rare congresses where there were more people on the last day than on the first. That congress gave flesh to the principles laid down in *Populorum Progressio*.

Populorum Progressio is one of the strongest papal documents of the twentieth century. Not only does it sum up and reiterate the Church's social teachings since Leo XIII's famous encyclical *Rerum Novarum*, but it breaks new ground in several areas. This is done in stirring and touching language — unusual for an encyclical.

Populorum Progressio was the first encyclical directed entirely to the issue of international development — and it makes it clear that peace is hollow unless based on *economic justice*. Real peace needs justice. This message flies in the face of that endless prattling about peace and violence which ignores the causes of violence. Paul then shows how this economic imbalance has been structured into society. People, without even knowing it, are part of a whole structure which, without any ill will or evil intentions on the part of those who run it, deals death to a large segment of society. Hence, we have evolving here the concept of structural sin, social sin, which now has become so central to theology.

Sin by its nature implies personal decision and culpability, whereas a structure by its nature, once it is set in place, is impersonal and, strictly speaking, is not capable of sin. That is why Pope Paul, in stressing the problem of sinful structures and situations, was careful not to eliminate *personal responsibility*. His point was that we must personally act to dismantle structures of sin. *Non-action becomes a choice, becomes sin, a personal sin*; it is at this moment that the word *sin* in the phrase *structural sin* ceases to be an analogy and becomes a sin in a genuinely imputable sense: our sin, my sin. And when we stand before God we must accuse ourselves not only of sin in the traditional sense but of the part we play actively or *by silence* in permitting the sort of structure which allows Negros to be a hell on earth for thousands of peasants.

Throughout the encyclical Paul's favorite word is *integral*: integral salvation, integral liberation, integral development. Integral is a touchstone of Catholic social teaching. It means that spiritual development considered totally apart from material development is a parody of the word spiritual. The result is a situation like Negros, where many devout landowners see the pursuit of holiness as unrelated to the challenge to change the structures of sin. It also means, conversely, that material development separated from spiritual values is equally destructive. Both aberrations are forms of reductionism, the sort of reductionism on which fundamentalists of every stripe thrive.

Paul finished the encyclical with a call to work for development—the integral development mentioned above—and then ended with the dramatic phrase: *Development is the new name for peace.* Thus the pope linked violence with the absence of a just order.

The encyclical contained a statement Fortich must have felt was written just for Negros: "When whole populations destitute of necessities live in a state of subjection barring them from all initiative and responsibility, and from all opportunities to advance culturally and to share in social and political life, men are easily led to violence to right these wrongs to humanity."

The message was clear: we in Negros should act now to preempt a violent cataclysm in the future.

Once that Rural Congress was over, the new bishop threw himself into the work of doing something for the poor of Negros. The list of programs and projects he started in those first years is formidable. The major items included:

— The implementation of land reform on Church properties.

— The opening of the Social Action Center.

— The appointment of Fr. Luis Jalandoni to take charge of the Social Action Center.

— The opening of negotiations for the purchase of an old sugar mill, then transferring it on a convoy of eighty trucks to a remote mountain valley and setting up the Dacongcogon Sugar, Rice and Corn Cooperative.

— The starting of a cottage industry to make cheap clothes for the cane-field workers who would do the work and get the profits from the project.

— The starting of a legal-aid scheme with two lawyers free for the poor.

— The setting up of a radio station and TV station to propagate the new thrust.

— The setting up of a folk-arts school at Busay.

— The allowing of Fr. Edgar Saguinsin and Fr. Hector Mauri to start the National Federation of Sugarcane Workers (NFSW).

— The setting up, with Bishop Cornelius De Wit of Antique on the neighboring island, of a scheme to liberate the *sacadas*, the migrant workers transported to Negros each year to cut the cane.

— The issuing of a pastoral letter on the rights of laborers and their present plight.

Probably most important of all, he convinced his own priests that service to the poor was essential to their ministry.

People often forget that in all these projects, and many others not mentioned, Fortich carried the rich *hacenderos* and businessmen along with him, infecting some of them with his enthusiasm and encouraging them to get involved. A great number joined him and helped with these projects. They had a debt of gratitude to him for his personal influence in their lives, exerted especially through the retreats he gave. He himself had a bit of magic as if maybe in some other life he had kissed the Blarney Stone and now was using this gift for all he was worth to cajole the elite of Negros into the struggle to change the social face of the island.

In those days the spacious old Spanish palace teemed with people of every sort. Fortich's office door was always wide open; groups of officials from this agency and that crowded in to hear words of encouragement from the bishop, who pushed them to try harder and to do something for the "little people." Social action groups seemed to be meeting in every corner of the palace and beggars found their way right into the bishop's room. Symposia, cooperatives, seminars and endless projects for social development were underway. Fortich had taken to heart Paul VI's slogan: Development is the new name for peace.

Development

The list above is divided roughly into two groups. Most of the projects were developmental, but some were also liberational. By developmental I mean that they put the emphasis on economic progress within the existing structures. By liberational I mean that they saw the structures themselves as the problem and in need of change. At the time, few of us were aware of this distinction. We were buoyed up with the idea of helping the poor. Somehow we did not realize just how much and what type of change would eventually be involved.

Of course the developmental and the liberative aspects can't always be neatly divided; some very good developmental projects are liberational and vice versa. But in those days we presumed that the basic economic and social structures were not a problem. The challenge was to help the poor to avail themselves of the opportunities *already there* of participating in the national wealth by setting up livelihood projects, for example, pig and duck breeding, the cooperative sugar mill, the workers clothing project. These would provide work and income and make small capital available to the ordinary people. To put it in another way, a developmental project meant helping people to increase their income, but not necessarily to change the plantation system or the dependent attitude bred by it.

Later on we came to realize that no developmental project was any good unless it *developed people*, unless people themselves grew and became self-reliant in the process. And later still we realized that any project, if it was for the long-term good of the people, must eventually lead to the dismantling or replacing or radical modification of those structures, such as the plantation system, which were the ultimate cause of the people's misery. When this happened, development and liberation embraced.

Meanwhile, the grandiose developmental schemes of the Asian Development Bank were aimed at developing *things*: roads, highways, infrastructures (for getting the wealth out!), but not people. Often these schemes resulted in the disempowerment of people, as in the case of some of the sugar mills backed by that bank. These mills were advertised as great acts of development, but in fact they involved the small holders losing their lands and becoming dependent first on the mill and eventually on world markets. This dependence was at the heart of the problem of the poor.

From Plantation to Mountain

Meantime I had gone to live on a sugar cane plantation — the one I mentioned earlier. There I got a worm's-eye view of how hacienda laborers lived. I began to translate *Populorum Progres-*

sio into Ilonggo, and suddenly the exhortations of the encyclical leapt to life amid the desperate reality of the plantation shacks. In fact, at times they even seemed too mild. So when the Roman Synod in 1971 produced the document *Justice in the World*, I felt the Magisterium was now finally saying it as it should be said: "Action on behalf of justice and participation in the transformation of the world fully appear to us as a constitutive dimension in the preaching of the gospel." That word constitutive — a scholastic term — was carefully chosen. In other words, no justice, no gospel. Religion without justice is truly opium. Religion without justice is Bad News.

But strangely enough, I still did not see the centrality of justice to the Old and New Testament. I would quote a piece here and there to back our stand for fair treatment for the laborers, but it was not till I moved to the mountains some years later that the scriptural basis of the struggle for justice came home to me.

In 1976 I was changed from the plantation to a parish in the mountains. It was a very different social situation. In the rich alluvial lowlands cane workers were tied to the plantations, but here in the mountain valleys where new land had been opened up with the cutting down of the forest, many poor settlers had hacked out a space for themselves to farm. Now they were being ousted from their hard-won holdings by influential lowlanders who used the military to terrorize them. Insurgency naturally thrived.

Here in the mountains I began to work with what were called the Basic Christian Communities. Reflecting on the scriptures plays a central role in these communities. For the first time I began to see the thread from Genesis and Exodus through the Prophets and the Psalms to the New Testament. God's people on the road to freedom — struggling toward the kingdom of peace and justice. I knew it theoretically before, but now I saw in a new light how the first Christians celebrated the death and resurrection of Jesus on the very feast that their ancestors celebrated the Passover from slavery to freedom.

Hence, the central act of worship of the Church, the Mass,

has at its heart a commemoration and rededication to that original and now expanded struggle for full human freedom. That is why the Mass, when properly understood, is nothing less than an act of revolution, a radical call for personal and social transformation; it challenges every unjust structure and calls us to offer our lives in the struggle to change these structures.

When the priest raises the chalice and says, "This is my blood, which will be poured out for you," and then adds, "Do this in commemoration of me," he is calling Christians not only to repeat the ritual but to repeat the original act: to offer their lives in the struggle for total freedom. In light of this, is it possible to be against social transformation and to be in the state of grace?

This central point of the Mass struck me — and the people — particularly on one occasion. My parish was on a rise across the Tablas river from Oringao, the parish of Fr. Brian Gore. One day I went to a distant village to say Mass, the first Mass in that particular Christian Community. Their little *kapilya* or chapel looked over the river to Brian's parish, which stretched beyond. Fr. Gore and six of his lay leaders had just been arrested and imprisoned on a false charge (not the killing of the mayor, which was to come later, but a lead-up charge to that). A grenade and bullets were planted in his office, and then he and his staff were accused of possessing illegal arms and subversive literature. This first arrest had frightened the new members of the Christian Community. That was why the gospel we chose was Mark 21:21: "You shall be arrested and taken before judges." I explained this simply for the new Christians; they were called to defend the poor and to stand up for their own dignity. The price would be what the gospel said: they would be brought before judges. This is what had happened to Christ because his actions were misunderstood as stirring up the people.

When I came to the consecration, I took up the host and said the ancient words: "This is my body, which is given up for you; this is my blood, which is shed for you." It seemed to me at that moment that the full meaning of being a disciple was clear to the people as it was becoming clearer to me.

This connection between the Mass and the Passover, between the Exodus theme in the Old Testament and the vision of the Basic Christian Communities made the Mass into a great challenge to confront the system. A far cry from the Mass of days past, said alone in a chapel for a stipend as a propitiatory sacrifice for the soul of someone unknown to the celebrant! The latter represented a Church hypnotized by death, the former a Church challenged by the realities of life. The Church in Negros had come a long way, and not everyone was happy with the journey.

Pope John Paul in Negros

Pope John Paul II came to Negros in January 1981, a few months before he was shot, almost fatally. Precisely because Negrenses were divided on where the Church stood, his words were awaited with tension. Almost three quarters of a million peasants massed on the huge area reclaimed from the sea near Bacolod Cathedral to hear him. The tension was heightened before the pope's arrival, when Imelda Marcos appeared and took the microphone prepared for the pope and told the throng that, contrary to reports in *Time* magazine, Negros was not an island of fear, but an island of joy. No one clapped. A little while later, the pope arrived.

I'd love to give all of his message, because here is a pope stepping onto an island where priests and the sons of *hacenderos* and doctors have joined a revolution now in progress precisely over social issues, so his words do have a special weight. Here are a few passages:

It is in the name of Christ, and because she must preach his message of love to the whole world, that the Church speaks out on behalf of the dignity of the whole of mankind, but in the first place of those who are most in need.

I repeat what I said once before: that "the world willed by God is a world of justice ... The dignity of man and

the common good of society demand that society be based
on justice.

There are in today's world too many situations of injustice.
Injustice reigns when some nations accumulate riches and
live in abundance while other nations cannot offer the
majority of people the basic necessities. Injustice reigns
when within the same society some groups hold most of
the wealth and power while large strata of the population
cannot decently provide for the livelihood of their families
even though they do long hours of backbreaking labor in
factories or in the fields. Injustice reigns when the laws of
economic growth and ever greater profit determine social
relations, leaving in poverty and destitution those that have
only the work of their hands to offer. *Being aware of such
situations, the Church will not hesitate to take up the cause
of the poor and to become the voice of those who are not
listened to when they speak up, not to demand charity, but to
ask for justice* (emphasis added).

It goes on and on. It was the pope's clearest statement on
where the Church stands on social matters in the Philippines.
There was one strange sequel. That night all of us priests joined
Bishop Fortich to celebrate the successful visit of the pope—no
assassination attempts, not even a hitch, and then the stunning
endorsement of our work. The phone in the corner of the room
rang; Bishop Fortich was called. He was out of earshot, but we
could see the sudden gravity of his face. When he put down the
phone he was reluctant to speak for a moment. Then he said,
"That was the head of the Sugar Planters' Association. He's
raging. He wants to know who wrote the pope's speech. And he
says if that's his message there'll be war in Negros!"

There already was war in Negros. The pope was giving the
Church's formula for peace.

Looking through the sources, biblical, patristic, and magisterial, it is clear that the Church's teaching is now unambiguous
with regard to the pursuit of justice: Christianity is grotesque

when it turns its back on justice. It's not Christianity. It's something else.

But the Church *is* ambiguous about the *methods* to be used to attain justice. Under certain conditions she does permit the use of counterviolence, for example, in the case of wars of national defense. But what of the decision of priests and other Christians, many of whom I have known, to take up arms in defense of an oppressed people? Was this decision justified in the light of this Church tradition? Is, therefore, the decision of Luis Jalandoni and other Christians to take up arms justifiable in the light of this Christian tradition?

[3]

Armed Struggle

Unlikely Revolutionaries

It is no secret that many Roman Catholic priests and some Protestant pastors on Negros have joined the armed struggle to change the social face of this island.

I knew most, if not all, of the priests. These priests were dedicated to their duty as priests, and some of them were outstanding. In watching them at work, in talking with them, at times in working with them I was taken by their personal sincerity, intelligence and dedication.

I knew many others who have joined too. There was Ana, who lived beside our little farm in Tabugon. She was sixteen years of age and the most beautiful girl around. She was only four feet ten inches tall, but she instantly stole your attention with her bright, intelligent eyes. She was a devout Baptist. The thought that someday she would be trekking through the mountain forests with a gun at her hip and leading a revolutionary educational team was, at that time, inconceivable. She was a frequent visitor to our cooperative farm experiment, and soon she fell in love with Marco Gomez, one of our co-op members. I witnessed their marriage in the parish church. Not long after they both made the decision to join the New Peoples Army. To do so, Ana had to go through a traumatic break with her father. She was the eldest of many children, had done well at school and was the financial hope of the family.

49

Ana had many children of her own during those years on the run — seven in all, including twins. Miraculously, they all lived, but every now and again I would receive desperate notes from a barefoot messenger in the middle of the night asking for medicine or help in secretly getting Ana to a clinic in the lowlands when a birth was difficult. I became godfather to one of those children.

While Ana, gun at her hip in case of ambush, gave seminars to the peasants, she and Marco never missed a chance to steal a visit to their children, who were by necessity billeted with foster mothers. These foster mothers were well aware of the dangers but offered their home to the children of the "red" fighters and treated these children as their own.

Ana would have explained her dream like this: to bring about a land where 70 percent of the children were not malnourished, where equal opportunity existed, where she could live with her own children in peace. The strategy was to stake out "liberated" areas in the inner mountains where the writ of the corrupt Marcos government did not prevail and the people could build a cooperative lifestyle. These were called "red" areas. Around these areas were zones which, though not controlled by the New Peoples Army, were nevertheless areas where the fighters could move freely. Eventually, after a long protracted struggle, the whole island and all the islands would be free. Meanwhile, for Ana, it was the mountains, eating roots for food, sleeping on the earth far from her children.

On one occasion Marco was caught and tortured mercilessly by a certain Lt. Lamayo in an attempt to get him to sign a document saying that Fr. Gore and I were recruiting for the NPA. Lamayo forced Marco to dig his own grave. "He placed me standing in that hole and covered my body up to the waist, pointing an M16 assault rifle at me and insisting that if I would not sign, I would die that very moment. In response I told him that it was better that he would shoot me, because I could not suffer any longer, but I would not sign the statement because I knew nothing about what he was saying. And that if he was afraid to fire a shot, because it would call attention, he could use his knife to end my life. Instead he twisted my head and executed karate chops on my shoulders. When he found out that I was already weak, he ordered his men to remove me from the hole and brought me to the barracks and again put a chain on my leg and locked me."[1] Marco miraculously escaped. He and Ana elected to continue the struggle in spite of what they knew could be their fate.

Then there was a catechist, Vilma, taken away in the middle of the night by the Philippine military to a "safe house." There she was tortured with electrodes till she went out of her mind. Though she recovered after some years, many of her large family joined the New Peoples Army.

There was Macao Gallardo, son of a leading doctor in Bacolod City and related to many of the planter families. His natural destiny would be to choose whatever academic course he wished and become part of the elite who ruled the island. He chose instead to join the NPA. (Once when his father was doing a small local operation on my foot, he approached when the nurse was out of earshot and whispered to me, "How's my son?" He presumed erroneously that since I was from a mountain parish I would have contact with him.)

Then there was Commander Garry, who had himself been a military man in Murcia. Disgusted with the behavior of his fellow soldiers he joined the NPA.

There was Virgie and Boy . . . I could keep listing names as the faces come up before me, but what I'm trying to say is that these were and are ordinary human beings — not the horned, red terrorists that army press reports describe. They were extraordinary only in that their concern and care for others went beyond their own personal families to the mass of peasants in Negros; they wanted a new heaven and a new earth.

Of course people like Ana and Marco didn't think things out in theological terms of the just-war theory. For people like them, in the words of Helder Camara, "injustice is the primary violence." This was their starting point. The peasants of Negros are undergoing violence through the massive injustice weighing on them; their armed struggle is not an initiation of violence but counter-violence. War had already been declared by the system; the people have responded in self-defense. The military's repressive response became, in turn, yet a *third* level of violence.

For priests like Luis Jalandoni the theological concept of the just-war theory was important. The active leadership of these priests, or at least their blessing, was a vital factor in strengthening the revolution in Negros, an island which is 90 percent Catholic and where the Church, in spite of everything, is still the most credible institution around.

Fr. Luis Jalandoni came from one of the landed families of Negros — one of several such families who have shown a social concern for the poor. He joined the seminary after finishing accountancy in one of the best colleges in the Philippines, the University of St. Lasalle. He was no young boy swept into the priesthood unthinkingly.

Fr. Luis had high intellectual ability, so after studying at the Angelicum in Rome, he was sent to post graduate studies at Munich in Germany under Karl Rahner. He came back to the Philippines with the central conviction that theology was like a gearshift that must be used to engage the believer with the engine of life, in this case the daily life of the peasants of Negros through whom his parents and his aunts and uncles gained their wealth.

Luis was light skinned and slight of build. He looked straight at you through rimless spectacles. His intensity was relieved by a little smile ever ready to play about his lips. He gave you his full attention, and if your conversation ended in making an appointment, he'd take from his pocket a minuscule notebook and in tiny writing carefully mark in the day and hour. His overall bearing could be summed up in one word: gentleness. Within a few months of his return from Germany he became the accepted leader among the priests of the diocese.

Apart from being intelligent, Luis was reticent and self-effacing. Maybe that was why Bishop Fortich, newly in office, asked him to head the Social Action Center and made him its first director.

Luis got going immediately. He helped Bishop Fortich set up

a sugar, rice and corn cooperative and mill in the mountains of Tabugon, where I was later parish priest. This involved huge bank loans and the buying of an old sugar mill and the shifting of the whole plant and equipment into the interior mountains. It took seventy trucks and myriad other vehicles, which formed a sort of caravan a kilometer long, to haul the mill over roads newly prepared. It was quite a sight, and Fortich, who blessed the caravan as it lined up at Bacolod Plaza before it left for the mountains, felt proud to be implementing the words of Paul VI: "Development is the new name for peace."

Luis also helped set up a large community farm called Ka-isahan in the mountains of Candoni at a place called Kanto-manyog. He helped get loans from the German bishops for the tractors and equipment. Luis also set up a free legal aid office for the poor.

At that time Jesuit Hector Mauri, with Fr. Edgar Saguinsin,[2] had helped start an independent labor union for the sugar workers. This union was called the National Federation of Sugar Workers (NFSW). Fr. Luis helped to strengthen the union by forming the Justice for Sugar Workers Committee, whose members were ordinary, respected citizens. They would support and back the union. I was a member. Luis, as I recall, was the chairman or executive secretary.

It was the free legal aid office that first led to trouble. A great number of poor peasants came to Fr. Jalandoni because their land was being grabbed by rich lowlanders. The ploy of some landowners, when a small-time sharecropper or settler got in their way, was to accuse him of some crime. The peasant would of course be jailed, and they would take his land; or the legal expenses would be too much for the poor man, who had problems in even getting shoes to appear at the court case. He would give up and eventually become a day laborer on land he had previously cleared. We are talking not about the good fertile lowlands, but the hilly land leading to the mountains or the valleys inside the mountains. We are talking about rich people with first-class land in the lowlands wanting more and so resorting to taking the food out of the mouths of the already struggling peasants in the interior. This is the sort of situation Amos the prophet had in mind.

Fr. Jalandoni took the cases to court and proceeded to lose case after case; I think he lost some four hundred cases. This in spite of the fact that he had a good, honest lawyer. Perhaps having an honest lawyer was not an asset. He had his family and relations beggared from borrowing their land titles to go surety for peasants out on bail. The reticent priest became articulate.

In 1971 trouble broke out on the three plantations owned by Victorias Milling Company north of Bacolod. The laborers worked to join the Federation of Free Farmers (FFF), but the company management blocked them. In August Fortich intervened and personally went to the management with a letter asking that no pressure be exerted on the workers and a free atmosphere be allowed to prevail till the certification election (an election in which laborers choose what union they want) would decide the matter.

However, the strike broke out and the picket started on August 13. The strike became a symbol for the plantation workers throughout the island. Many priests and sisters appeared on the picket line and a Mass on the line was scheduled for September 11. The bishop was not in favor of the Mass. He felt his role as mediator between the two sides would be compromised. As eleven priests were vesting for the Mass, a telegram arrived. Fr. Jalandoni opened it. It was from Bishop Fortich: "I do not authorize the saying of the Mass on the picket line." There was silence. Fr. Dimitri Gatia and Fr. Romeo Empestan said they couldn't go ahead if the bishop did not approve. Luis countered by saying: "I have good reasons for disagreeing with the bishop, but there is no time to go into it. The workers are all waiting." There was a moment of indecision, then an old priest, Fr. Crispin Ruiz, said, "To hell with it—we'll say the Mass."

Luis began to ask larger and larger questions. Was there any purpose in the legal system beyond helping the rich to take from the poor? Did the government labor court, set up to fix disputes between landowners and laborers, ever act in favor of the laborers? He delved into the history of it all, going back to the Revolution in 1898, when the Negros elite had refused to join General Emilio Aguinaldo in his insurrection against Spain. Instead Negros had, under the lead of some planters, declared itself *independent* from the rest of the Philippines in order to protect its sugar industry.[3] Finally, the same sugar planters had raised the Stars and Stripes and declared for the United States *even before the American gunboats arrived.*[4] It was clear to Luis that Negros was organized around sugar by the sugar barons; its institutions were there not to give justice but to keep this system in place.[5]

He began to read the writings of the more militant Filipino heroes. I recall Luis reading to me with excitement a passage he had recently discovered in the writings of Andres Bonifacio. Bonifacio had specifically chosen armed struggle as the means to expel the Spaniards. But he had been traitorously executed by other members of the revolution, who wanted the Spaniards to go but did not want a social revolution within the Philippines. They wanted to take the place of the Spaniards; eventually they did.

One day when Luis was visiting a large hacienda in Negros Oriental, where the laborers had gone on strike, he witnessed a terrible sight: hired goons of the landlord fired directly at the laborers while town police stood by. Luis leaped for the ditch with the others. As the bullets ripped over his head, the awful realization hit him: There is no legal way to fight this evil.

The last straw for Luis was the declaration by President Ferdinand Marcos of martial law on September 21, 1972. From that moment, it was clear that no legal attempt at reform would be allowed and President John Kennedy's prophecy would be fulfilled: "Those who make reform impossible make revolution inevitable." Luis and hundreds like him went to the hills.

The Just-War Theory

From Luis's point of view, and that of so many priests and educated lay people who led the revolution all over the Philippines, this was a classic case of the just-war just-revolution theory. The decision to take up arms, though it may have been forced on him, was for Luis in line with Catholic teaching. He knew his theology. For him the conditions were present in which traditional Catholic thinking would allow one to take up arms.

Of course, one of the weaknesses of the just-war theory is that those most involved in the outcome are the ones making the assessment. Was Luis's assessment correct? Were the peasants, are the peasants of Negros in a position analogous to the oppressed colonists in America when they took up arms against mother England? Or the oppressed peasants of France when they rose up against Louis XVI? It's a question that must be answered by anyone who lives in a similar revolutionary situation. This question must be answered by anyone who takes the Negros situation seriously.

Ordinary Christians don't often take time out to examine the morality of war; war comes upon them unexpectedly and for most, the decisions are out of their hands. When they do examine the morality of war they discover that the legitimacy of war and revolution is one of the few doctrines that all the mainline Christian Churches, all the major religions, indeed all the principal world views agree on. They all agree that under certain circumstances war or revolution is legitimate.

Killing, they say, is not always wrong.

But since the New Testament precludes killing, without qualification, Christians have been at pains to justify exceptions and have therefore developed the theology of the just war or just revolution, though this after is a relatively late development.

The early expansion of the Christian Church after the death of the apostles tended to be among slaves and subject peoples of the Roman Empire. These early Christians had no say in the running of the empire; they were the underdogs. They practiced pacifism, and evidence shows that soldiers, when they became Christians, had to choose between their two callings; being a soldier and being a Christian were not compatible.[6]

There was an added reason why Christians were persecuted so much and seen almost as enemies of the state. It was precisely because they were not prepared to defend it with arms; they were in effect pacifists. Then one of the most important events in the history of Christianity took place.

In the year 324, following the Edict of Milan in 312, the Emperor Constantine lifted the ban on Christianity. Christians could now emerge from hiding and take their place in governing the empire. Should they also take their place in the defense of the empire, in the wars of the empire?

Fifth-century theologian Augustine of Hippo saw the dilemma—the tension between the right to defend oneself and the sacredness of life. In a later age Albert Camus would formulate the dilemma thus: "How to be neither victims nor executioners." The dilemma was severe for Christians precisely because Christ forbade killing and demanded that we *love* our enemies. How then could Christians defend the empire—an empire which had become *our* empire? And the barbarians were at the gates.

Augustine came up with the just-war theory. He carefully enumerated several conditions under which Christians could bend the gospel teachings against killing and take part in war, could kill. If these conditions were present, the war was deemed just. Throughout the centuries this theory has been refined by Christian theologians, who have molded and changed the necessary conditions for this just war. They call it a "limit" situation, an "interim ethic." Theologians disagree on the number and nature of the conditions. In *Five Classic Just-War Theories*, LeRoy Walters shows there are five different theories—apart, that is, from Augustine's.[7]

If you go into the moral theology section of a great library and work through the most famous names for the last two centuries under the heading of just war, you will find that the theory is alive and well.

So much for the theologians; the Churches themselves, with the exception of the small peace Churches like the Quakers and the Mennonites, to this day accept the just-war theory and freely send chaplains to minister to and even encourage the troops.

They allow the chaplains to wear military uniform with rank

and insignia, carry military titles and, in some cases, as in the Philippines, at times to carry guns. The soldiers even form a specific "diocese" with a bishop of their own. (When Luis was later captured, an army chaplain was used to interrogate him and to try and break him down. Luis told him he was betraying his priesthood.)

One of the strange things about the theory of the just war was that in practice it was not applied to insurrection, uprising, revolt or revolution *against an existing government*. Hence, in the early formation of the theory there was always a preoccupation with the question, Who has the right to declare war? These formulations of the theory rarely gave that right to an oppressed group *within* the state.

In this same tradition we have the strong Church condemnation, for almost a hundred years after the event, of the French Revolution, which took place in 1789, and the Church's position in the treaty of Vienna in 1815, in favor of restoring the original monarchial regimes toppled by Napoleon. This tradition found its way down to recent times in the general reaction of always backing the de facto government, no matter how cruel or unjust it was. With "stability" there was hope. With revolution society entered a dark chaotic tunnel with maybe a worse situation at the other end.

That changed in 1967 with the publication of *Populorum Progressio*. *Populorum Progressio* is a historic document for many reasons, but particularly for paragraph 31:

> We know, however, that a revolutionary uprising — save where there is manifest, long-standing tyranny which would do great damage to fundamental rights and dangerous harm to the common good of the country — produces new injustices, throws more elements out of balance and brings on new disasters. A real evil should not be fought against at the cost of greater misery.

For the first time in magisterial teaching, the just-war theory was broadened and specifically applied to the internal revolutionary situation, though with qualifications. Leo XIII had said that in the last resort Christians must endure injustices rather than rebel. Donal Dorr says, apropos of paragraph 31, "It is clear that, faced with the same ultimate choice as that which faced Leo XIII, Pope Paul refused to take the same position."[8]

Paragraph 31 of *Populorum Progressio* was one of the most quoted and most often appealed to papal teachings during the next twenty years in the Third World because it was precisely in places like Latin America, the Philippines and Africa that people felt these conditions applied. It would not be an exaggeration to say that this paragraph played an important role in gaining the sympathy and tolerance of the Catholic Church toward revolutionary movements at this time. The debate was no longer whether it was right or wrong to revolt; it was about whether the conditions for revolution were fulfilled. The term *revolutionary situation* took on a special meaning, no longer representing simply a description of the situation but connoting a moral judgment that this was a situation in which revolution was justified. At national gatherings in the Philippines, religious bodies passed resolutions saying that the Philippines was in a revolutionary situation. Those who read that as a mere description missed the full implication. It meant that the conditions for a just revolution mentioned in paragraph 31 of *Populorum Progressio* were present.

This heightened debate around paragraph 31 of *Populorum Progressio* might lead one to expect a statement from the Vatican which would seek to dampen the enthusiasm. Not so. The next important teaching statement on that specific topic, the document "Instruction on Christian Freedom and Liberation" (March 1986), reiterated this teaching. Though not on the same level as an encyclical, it was a special teaching instrument awaited by the Third World with great anticipation. The heading is significant: "A Last Resort."

These principles must be especially applied in the extreme case where there is recourse to armed struggle, which the Church's magisterium admits *as a last resort* to put an end to an obvious and prolonged tyranny which is gravely damaging to the fundamental rights of individuals and the common good. Nevertheless, the concrete application of these means cannot be contemplated until there has been a very rigorous analysis of the situation (no. 79) (emphasis added).

Apart from the official Magisterium of the Church, which clearly approves counter-violence as a last resort, there is, since the age of Constantine in the fourth century, a continual history of the practical approval by the Church of the use of violence. For example:
— The relaxing of the older Church teaching (pre-Constantine) of not serving in armies.
— The Crusades, which were blessed by the Church.
— The introduction of papal armies to defend the Papal States.
— The approval of the death penalty in times of the Inquisition and under less cruel circumstances down to our own day.
— The religious wars of Europe.
— The approval of army chaplains down to our own times. Chaplains being allowed to hold rank and wear uniforms and sometimes carry arms.
— The absence of any official Church ruling or guidelines on investing in armaments or paying taxes to support wars.
— The absence of significant magisterial teaching on torture, a crime which some theologians regard as morally worse than killing, and one of the great crimes of our age.
This pro-war bias surely was helped by the Old Testament tradition, which is replete with examples of the Chosen People using arms, with God's approval, to attain what they needed for survival.
Some arguments are used from the New Testament to show that Christ approved the use of the sword, but they are isolated texts — the most common being the cleansing of the temple. Such arguments hardly stand up to scholarly scrutiny. There is no serious attempt among scripture scholars today to say that the New Testament approves counter-violence.

Conditions for Just Revolution

The above arguments in favor of counter-violence come from authority of one sort or another, whether official church teaching, history or the scriptures. But the ordinary people who make the decisions to use violence as a last resort do not normally make their decision based on the above arguments. Rather, they perceive the decision as one of common sense and use those arguments to justify it. As a common-sense decision, there are two formulations:

Personal Self-Defense: All women and men have a right to defend themselves and their families from an unjust aggressor who is about to kill them, even if that means killing the aggressor.

Group Self-Defense: Just as individuals have the right to defend themselves, a group has the right to defend itself when threatened with death. If the group has this right, then it has the prior right to prepare for this event and move into action when the danger is imminent and likely.

Based on the above, those who hold for the just-war and just-revolution theory believe that, as a last resort, counter-violence is justified and may even be obligatory under certain conditions. It is necessary to examine these conditions, at least briefly, but first we must recall that there has never been any universal agreement on the conditions for a just war. They have changed from age to age and theologian to theologian. The conditions given here are based on *Populorum Progressio* and the *Instruction on Christian Freedom and Liberation*:

1) a prolonged tyranny;

2) an obvious tyranny;

3) a gravely damaging tyranny;

4) a tyranny destructive of personal human rights and the common good;

5) the evil of the war to be started must not outweigh the evil being suffered;

6) the war must be a last resort.

A Prolonged Tyranny: This provision is in order to avoid start-ing a cycle of revolutions before there is any chance to give gradualism and reformism a chance. It aims at avoiding a swing-ing from revolution to revolution.

Obvious Tyranny: This provision is vague. What is obvious to someone suffering its effects may not be obvious to someone not so affected. However, the intent of the provision is to ensure some degree of common agreement on the existence of the tyr-anny in question.

Gravely Damaging: All societies are societies of varying degrees of tyranny on some part of the population. A decision has to be made as to where the bearable threshold is. Hence the provision gravely damaging.

Damaging to the Common Good: Damage is not just to indi-viduals, but to the common good, to the society as a whole.

Balance of Damage: The damage done through a prolonged war or revolution must be balanced against the damage being done by the tyranny. This is not an easy assessment to make. If a short, sharp war is possible, then it could do less damage to society and the fabric of society than continued suffering of an existing unjust regime.

As a Last Resort: The theory presumes that all other reason-able means have been tried.

Such are the conditions given today for a just revolution.

A significant number of the people of Negros, looking at these conditions for a just revolution, say that they have been verified in Negros for some time now. Let us see what they claim about each condition.

Just-War Theory Applied to Negros

Prolonged Tyranny: They claim the present tyranny is pro-longed. It, in fact, began with the second colonizing of the island of Negros in the middle of the nineteenth century. This caused the destruction and dispersal of much of the local population, and the driving to debt slavery of the remainder, along with the new peasantry brought in from the island of Panay and else-where. As the record shows, there has been a progressive dete-rioration for the peasants from being small landowners to being sharecroppers to being day laborers to debt slavery. In recent times destitution and soup kitchens are not uncommon. For over one hundred years the conditions have been getting progres-sively worse for more and more people, notwithstanding the periodic flowering and prospering of the cities.

Obvious Tyranny: They claim that this tyranny is highly visible; journalists and other observers from all over the world concur, so that Negros has become a symbol of injustice among organ-izations which attempt to help the Third World.

A considerable number of priests have left their ministry and joined the revolution. Considering that priests normally repre-sent the most conservative section of society, the fact that any of their number join the revolution is significant. These men have not gone to the New Peoples Army on the spur of the moment. There have been long years of soul searching. Those who take this step know that many priests have been killed and tortured in the Philippines for being vocal on human rights,[9] not to mention joining the revolution. So their decision demands courage.

Gravely Damaging: They claim that the damage is so great that grave damage is an understatement. With the present lack of food, we are in danger of having a generation of mentally retarded children due to malnutrition, a people whose sense of self-reliance will have been destroyed by having to line up for handouts, to enter prostitution or to beg in order to survive.

Damaging to the Common Good: They claim that the damage is not just to individuals. Whole communities have succumbed to a culture of poverty, a culture of fear, a culture of degrading dependency.

Evil of war outweighs the evil of the tyranny: They claim that many peasants are saying that it is more noble and more accept-able to die fighting rather than to die of hunger.

Either way, it will be a forced death. The history of what has been happening shows no light at the end of the tunnel. Things will only get worse; therefore, fighting gives dignity and hope where there is despair. With a longer time frame, the same decision faces the peasants as faced the Jews in the ghetto of Warsaw during the Second World War, when the order had been made to wipe them out. Why wait? If there is a decision not to change the present social structures, which over the last hundred years have caused so much misery, then that is a decision for mass death. Any who could emigrate would, but other countries will not take them. The United States will only take nurses and doctors and professionals, not the huddled masses.

As a Last Resort: Finally, they say this is our last resort. We have waited a hundred years. We have tried the political system of elite democracy, but that has offered us nothing. We have tried asking for changes; we have been outmaneuvered. We have tried asking for minimal land reform; so far, the majority of landholders will not give an inch, though they have held the land for years and years and have already grown rich from it. Using their power in the Congress, they watered down the Comprehensive Land Reform Law till its very sponsors walked out and voted against it. They have manipulated the watered-down version, getting enormous sums of money for useless land, for example, in the outrageous Garchitorena land deal. In this case the Department of Agrarian Reform purchased for sixty million pesos a piece of rocky land worth three million pesos. This monstrous burden was to be paid back by the receiving peasants over thirty years. In effect, the money borrowed abroad for land reform was thus being shared out among certain landlords who still did not give up their good land. The effect of all this is that after vast expenditure no sugar land worth talking about has been divided.

Based on the above, a significant number of Negrenses have been convinced that all the conditions traditionally required by the just-war theory are present; therefore, a stage has been reached, they say, where it is morally justifiable to take up arms against the unjust system which causes the present tyranny. These Negrenses come from across the whole class spectrum of Negros. They are the sons and daughters of *hacenderos*, of doctors and other professionals, of business people, of government officials. Some are priests; most are peasants. They have come to the conclusion that the island is in a situation of institutional violence and that they are justified morally in resorting to arms. They did not come to this conclusion because of an a priori faith in communism, though they have used Marxist ideology to achieve their ends. They came to it for the same reason that Americans in 1776, under much milder oppression, made the decision to revolt against the British using armed struggle. They have came to this conclusion for the same reason that the French made the decision to revolt against the aristocratic order of Louis XVI in 1789. These Negrenses are in a minority, though they now have a significant following who to a greater or lesser degree understand the logic of their leaders. They agree with their decision for armed revolution though the time may not, for strategic reasons, be ripe for a renewed attempt at the present time.

The Philippine military by arming local vigilante groups, by burning and shelling the mountains and corralling the people into hamlets have quieted the revolution. Many parts of the mountains and inner valleys are now deserted; the lid is firmly back on the pot again.

I recall one occasion when some of my friends—priests and sisters and former seminarians—in a gentle way asked me to join the armed struggle. I recall my discomfort; I was aware of the integrity of their lives and simplicity of their lifestyle, even their gentleness. I was aware of my own physical fear of taking such a step. I was aware that as Church teaching stood there was a credible moral argument for taking up arms. I was aware that should they succeed in bringing about a new age I would rejoice in it and benefit from it without having made any sacrifice myself.

But I was also aware, deep down, that I dreamed of a different road—the one of Gandhi, Martin Luther King, Dorothy Day, Daniel Berrigan, whose thoughts I had been exposed to through many years reading *The Catholic Worker* and *Fellowship*, the journal of the Fellowship of Reconciliation, of which I was a member. My embarrassment or my humiliation was keener because I was aware too that though I preached active nonviolence I still had nothing I could show for it. Of that gentle idealistic group of six with whom I spent some happy days in my house, three are now dead.

Marco is also dead. Marco and Ana for a while lived a seminormal life in a village which was "liberated." There they lived with their children and from there they carried on their organizing. One day Marco was sighted by the 7th Infantry Battalion not far from their home. They fired on him, and he was wounded. He crawled into the bushes, but they followed him.

When his little boy Toto found his father lying in the bushes his head had been severed from his body by a knife. Macao, the doctor's son, has resigned. Others are in exile. When we get together and list the people we knew, it's a long tale of death and torture, sometimes of resignation, surrender and even cases of betrayal. These people are not superior beings, just a very special cross section of humanity who cared enough to risk everything in a desperate bid to wipe the tears from the face of Negros.

The revolution simmers on; the institutional violence is still in place; the remote causes are unchanged. The majority of Negrenses who suffer from this institutional violence have never made a decision for armed struggle; they have made a different decision, a different option, though indeed they are not consciously aware that they have taken this other option. Yet this other option of theirs is ultimately the critical one for Negros and seals her fate.

[4]

Silence

The Ultimate Political Act

The Constitutional Convention

The sumptuous Manila Hotel, a queen among the hotels of Asia, lies outside the walls of the old Spanish city of Intramuros, now part of Manila. It was built for the new American overlords of the Philippines in 1912, and it was there that the great social events of the early American colonial years took place. It was there too that the first Constitutional Convention of the Philippines took place in 1935.

The purpose of this convention was to prepare the Philippines for self-rule as a democracy. The idea was that the drawing up of the Constitution would not be imposed by the Americans but written by a convention dominated by Filipinos, albeit Filipinos who had now been trained for thirty-five years in American-style democracy. After the promulgation of the convention, there would be a ten-year transition period — called the Commonwealth — and that would be followed by full freedom with the inauguration of the Philippine Republic in 1946.

Of course, the new Constitution favored the United States and favored the sugar block of Negros; it reflected the power realities of the time. However, the constitution did contain a provision which laid down that after thirty-five years there would be another Constitutional Convention. The delegates to this convention would be elected democratically from the people, and it would have the opportunity in the light of the intervening years of self-rule to amend and rewrite the Constitution of the Philippines.

In 1971 that convention was due. I was chaplain to a large sugar mill in Negros at that time. There was excitement in the air. Many ordinary people, even executives in the mill, had the idea that this Constitutional Convention would do something for the poor, particularly in Negros; it would be high on social justice. A group of executives from the sugar mill, due to their involvement in the Christian Family Life Movement, caught the idea that religion could not be separated from life and began to give small seminars on the upcoming convention. One of their slogans was "Man does not live by bread alone, but he does live by bread; we must provide that bread. We must have a Constitution which makes this possible."

All over the Philippines similar social awareness was growing. Student groups like KHI RHO or Kabataang Makabayan were proliferating; the Federation of Free Farmers was pushing for agrarian reform, particularly in the area of sharing the rice crop more equitably between the land tiller and the landowner. New genuine labor unions were coming to life. The Church was getting involved. Students were picketing Cardinal Santos for owning a bank; seminarians were on that picket line. People were hoping that social concerns would find a place somewhere in the Constitution.

Bishop Fortich issued his first pastoral letter on labor relations and the minimum wage around this time. In the sugar mill I had it mimeographed and gave copies to the labor union. To my surprise they, or at least their leader, were not interested. Of course, I was naively unaware that the union was controlled by the management and that its contract with management was what is called a sweetheart contract, which means the management dictates most of the terms. With the rebuff from the union, I was happy that executives who were members of the Christian

Family Life Movement were showing interest in the upcoming Constitutional Convention.

Then something happened. As preparations began for the election of delegates to the Constitutional Convention, a list of eight names appeared. It was called the Magic 8. These eight men were conservative sugar block supporters who would ensure that no change in the new constitution would endanger the power of the sugar barons of Negros. Word came down from the big sugar people in Bacolod that they wanted these men elected. I expected a fight, but I was wrong. The sugar mill let it be known to employees that they would have to vote for the Magic 8. The reaction was immediate; the little band of idealists crumpled. We heard no more about reform, and seven of the Magic 8 were elected.

The Manila Hotel had long fallen into neglect, but it was considered the proper venue for the Second Constitutional Convention, so it was refurbished and the convention opened there in February 1971.

From the start Marcos tried to suborn the convention. Considering the way the Negros delegates were elected, it would seem that that would not have been too difficult. But in spite of envelopes stuffed with money, some delegates were stubborn and pushed for social and economic reform on many fronts. The public debate was contagious and fueled a countrywide debate on nationalism and reform on every campus and street corner.

At dawn on September 21, 1972, Marcos put an end to all such discussion. He arrested his leading opponents. He closed the two houses of Legislation: the Senate and the Congress. He arrested leading senators like Jose Diokno and Benigno Aquino. He padlocked all the newspapers and imprisoned editors of at least two: Chino Roces of the *Manila Times* and Teodoro Locsin of the *Free Press.* One newspaper was left to continue: *The Daily Express* of Roberto S. Benedicto, the future sugar king of Negros. His television stations alone were left open. The manager of the mill where I was chaplain had the honesty to say to me: "This martial law, Father, is of course basically in favor of us" — meaning the sugar people.

Referendum — Plebiscite

The Constitutional Convention was reconvened once martial law was in place; members were offered a place in a new Interim National Assembly (which would take the place of the Congress and the Senate) if they would approve a new draft of the Constitution. This new draft was basically written in Malacañang, the president's palace. This draft contained what were called the *transitory provisions*; these clauses allowed Marcos to rule as a dictator at will with no time limits.

As everyone knew, by the law of the first Constitution this new Constitution would have to be approved by a plebiscite called specifically for the purpose. But Marcos announced a thing which he called a referendum-plebiscite. It would take place in the schools all over the country, and children of fifteen years of age and older were to participate. These gatherings would be called citizen assemblies. These citizen assemblies asked the onlookers several questions:

1. Did they approve the new Constitution with its carte blanche transitory provisions?
2. Did they still want a plebiscite other than this (as had been required by the Constitution)?
3. Should the Interim National Assembly be convened? (The delegates who approved this new Constitution were promised that they would sit in this assembly.)

The answers were not to be written but given by raising hands or viva voce, yea or nay. To Question One, the new controlled media reported fourteen million (90 percent of the electorate) answered yes. They approved the new Constitution with its transitory provisions. (There was no chance even to distinguish between approving it with or without those provisions.)

No. They did not want a plebiscite.

No. They did not want the new Interim National Assembly to be convened. Marcos would rule alone.

It was all over. The people had "democratically" ratified the new Constitution with its transitory provisions allowing Marcos's one-man rule and, according to this referendum-plebiscite, the voters did not want a rival to him in the form of the Interim National Assembly. (One wonders how those delegates felt who had voted for the transitory provisions precisely because it would allow them to sit in the Interim National Assembly — a magnificent double-cross!)

Martial law with its subsequent massive death and destruction in all parts of the Philippines and its consequent chronic war situation involving millions of lives found its legal basis on this castrated Constitutional Convention and the so-called referendum-plebiscite.

That referendum-plebiscite depended primarily on the submissive, obedient, passive compliance of school teachers and petty officials around the country. Without this compliance it would have been impossible. No Nazi tactics were used; no tanks rumbled in the streets. Some cooperated out of the desire for personal preferment; some complied out of the fear that promotion might be delayed. Most consented at least by silence and apathy or an unvoiced or unconscious evaluation that martial law ultimately placed their foot more firmly on the neck of the person below them. Of course, there were notable exceptions, all the more praiseworthy because they were in such a tiny minority.

Silence can be a political act. Silence in this case was a careful political act, a devastating political act. In subsequent years, when the full intent of Marcos was clear, the teachers still made no worthy protest against martial law as such; nor did they do so when the textbooks from grade one through the fourth year of high school were rewritten, or when they were asked to teach the banal "New Society" doctrine, which gave a spurious philosophical underpinning to the Marcos dictatorship.[1]

Someday some scholars are going to have to present this silence in a way that will shock the nation, because until that happens we will still enjoy the poisonous luxury of blaming Marcos and his cronies for the evil that resulted.

Silence as a Political Act

A similar event had taken place in Norway thirty years earlier, which Gene Sharp carefully documented. It is worthwhile comparing the two events, at least in certain respects.

In 1942, while the Nazi forces occupied Norway, the president of Norway, Vidkun Quisling, himself a fascist, set out to change Norway into a corporative state modeled on fascist Italy. He decided to start first with the teachers, they being the key to changing the minds of the young, and he announced that the teachers would be the "First Corporation."

The teachers protested. Between eight and ten thousand of the twelve thousand teachers wrote to Quisling saying they would not cooperate with the plan to change the education of the children to a fascist model, nor would they join the new teachers association.

The suffering to which Quisling and his troops subjected the teachers is part of Norwegian history, but the teachers never gave in and eventually Quisling was forced to abandon the plan. Hitler himself conceded defeat. The schools went back to the old model.[2]

In Germany, however, Hitler did succeed in killing six million Jews. He could not have done so without the cooperation of thousands of ordinary citizens. Someone had to do the paperwork, design and build the gas chambers, manufacture the Zyclon B gas and drive the trains. More important still, he needed the silent consent of millions of German Christians. Historians now agree that if Christians of all denominations had set their minds against the genocide of the Jews, it could not have taken place.

There is no doubt that silence has been the most devastating political act of the twentieth century.

Silence is the most important political factor in Negros, too. It is too easy to blame the *hacenderos*. True, they are the most visible element in the system, but in the first place, they are only one cog in the wheel of the sugar industry, and at times they themselves are victims.[3]

There are the sugar mills. They ask no questions about where the cane comes from or under what conditions it was cut, and they push for the highest share they can get. There are the bankers backed by the World Bank. They provide each year's crop loan, without which the hacienda could not continue; they never ask if borrowers are paying the minimum wage. There are the bank's investors throughout the world, who share some responsibility for how the interest on their money is earned. Nowadays there are plenty of ethical schemes, which will guarantee your money is not being spent to finance plantations or anything that you do not approve. When New York State pension funds withdrew their money from South Africa, others followed suit. The move had repercussions in South Africa, which began to take the first significant steps away from apartheid. Finally, there are the international traders; the final price for sugar is decided far from the Philippines.

These are all joint perpetrators and collaborators, but none of them could operate without the consent of the ordinary people.

The sugar industry in Negros employs some 300,000 laborers—this number rises and falls over the years with the fluctuations of the world market—and those workers have some one and a half million dependents.[4] Their consent is needed for the industry to continue. They form a base of the pyramid; if they walked away, the structure would fall. Granted, they couldn't walk away, but they do at least have the possibility of bargaining. Yet for the most part, they hold their tongues. It has been an uphill battle for any genuine labor union to organize the laborers.

If I step on your foot and you don't shout, are you not encouraging me to continue? Too often the laborers do not shout. So the laborers are guilty too. The silence on the plantations is eerie, pervasive, like a lonely desert.

I lived on a plantation for almost five years; not many foreign priests have had that experience. I had a worm's-eye view of what was going on, and this was definitely one of the better farms. The farm was owned by a landlord who had inherited it from his grandparents. He lived quietly in Manila, a humble, industrious man. The farm was one of several plantations owned by him. All of his plantations were run by one administrator. This was a cruel man. Each individual plantation had an *encargado* or overseer. The overseer on the plantation where I worked was kindly in character but single-minded in his determination, in his devotion, to doing whatever the administrator or the owner wanted. Under him were some *cabos* or gangers. I got to know one of them well, because he attended a Christian family group which I had started. We often discussed the injustices of the *encargado* and the administrator. I said to the *cabo* often: someday you will be the *encargado*. I hope you will not treat the laborers the way this man treats you. In due time he did become overseer and was worse than his predecessor. He was ruthless with the workers. He took a second woman, which meant he needed more money, and that meant more injustices on the farm.

Now, the interesting part is that the laborers who had known him all along never protested. The overseer's whole sense of personal worth depended on the social acknowledgment of the laborers of his position. There was the possibility of boycotting him socially. I suggested such nonviolent means as social ostracism but the laborers could never bring themselves to do that. They were prepared to talk about him behind his back, maybe even to knife him if things got too bad. But they were not prepared to confront him, though they would have been happy if I had done it for them. But I had made that mistake too often before and now answered with the old Ilonggo proverb: You are the ones being bitten but you want me to be the one to cry out.

The passivity of the cane workers has seeped into their bloodstream. Three different cultural strands come together to reinforce it. First, there is the feudal tradition going back to *before* the colonization, when debt slavery was heavily practiced in Philippine tribal life. Then there is the culture of poverty: who will dare bite the hand that feeds it? And third, there is the seasonal nature of sugar farming, which means the laborers are always in debt and thus lose any initiative in life. They wait and hope, and hope and wait. They take refuge in fatalism, masked by spurious theology: "It's the will of God. There is nothing we can do to change our situation."

Further, the sugar industry in Negros could not continue for a day without a small army of scriveners and officials and shopkeepers and engineers and agriculturists and bureaucrats and doctors, who make up the greater part of the middle class of Negros. These in turn are served by teachers, clergy and media. (These latter three groups fulfill a very special function, which I will deal with later.) For many years, with notable exceptions, the silence of this middle class was deafening. They walked the streets of the towns and cities unmindful or unaware or unconcerned that the whole pyramid of life in Negros depended on that peasant sugar base toiling away in the midday fields for wages that they themselves would laugh at. Their silence is more blameworthy than that of the sugar workers. Just as fish in the sea are not aware of the water—it takes someone on the shore to see the water—so the peasants have known nothing other than their present wretched life. But those standing on the shore can see how wrong their situation is.

It is this silence over the years that has made it possible for the Negros situation to continue, and it is the Church's breaking this silence which has caused dismay in the middle class and has earned the Church the wrath and even the hate of so many of the ruling class.

I have been contending that passivity of different sorts is actually the most important single factor in the Negros scene. I would like to spend a little time in examining the deeper reasons behind this.

Two Models of the Source of Power

Our experience of the role of passivity in holding an oppressive situation together is borne out by the studies of Gene Sharp in the first volume, *Power and Struggle,* of his three volume work, *The Politics of Nonviolent Action.* According to Sharp, there are two basic ways of looking at power in the world. The first sees power as coming from above. The second sees power as coming from below. Sharp goes into these two theories in depth. The first theory holds that power is monolithic; the people depend on the goodwill of the leader. The leader keeps the power intact by means of an army. Examples would be many dictatorships of Latin America, Eastern Europe before 1989, South Africa and the Philippines under Marcos.

The second theory is that power comes from below, from the people themselves, and if the people withdraw their consent then the ruler can rule no longer. Those who accept this second model of power as closer to the truth, as I do, understand the importance of silence, the importance of consent. Up till the People Power event in Manila in 1986, the modern classic example of this was the overthrow of the Shah of Iran. In 1979 the people withdrew consent, and he was left powerless in spite of the total backing of America and a huge well-equipped and well-trained army.

While I was writing this book (and after I had written the previous paragraph), we watched the powers in much of Eastern Europe collapse as the people simply withdrew their consent. The people did this sometimes by just walking away, sometimes by massing in the streets, sometimes symbolically by lighting millions of candles.

The idea that power actually depends on the consent of the people is so important that it has been said that it is, in the order of socio-political ideas, as earthshaking as Einstein's discovery of relativity has been in the order of science. In *Power and Struggle* Sharp shows that this theory has been around for some time. He quotes from Etienne La Boetie, a sixteenth-century French writer who wrote in *Discourse on Voluntary Servitude*: "He who abuses you has only two eyes, has but two hands, one body, and has naught but what has the least man of the great and infinite number of your cities, except for the advantage you give him to destroy you."[5]

Gandhi held the same view; namely, that "the maintenance of an unjust or nondemocratic regime is dependent upon the cooperation, submission and obedience of the populace."[6]

Gandhi's contemporary at the time he was thinking these thoughts was none other than the Filipino Jose Rizal—the inspiration behind the Philippine revolt against the Spaniards. Whether Jose Rizal ever heard of Gandhi's activities we don't know, but he came up with the same idea when he said: "There are no tyrants where there are no slaves."

Precisely because the theory that power emanates from the ruler is spurious, it needs continually to be bolstered: "The theory can only alter reality when both the subjects and the opponents of the regime presenting this monolithic image can be induced to believe the theory."[7] Hence, the vital need for those who use this model to control people's minds and therefore the essential part that religion, media, and schools play in keeping this model in position. They play a pivotal role because they legitimize the situation. They are a keystone in the edifice.

Our experience in the Philippines proves that the silence of the teachers was a major factor in the whole of the martial law process, and our experience in Negros shows that the silence of priests and teachers is necessary if Negros is to be kept a land of plantations with obedient, subservient and most of all quiescent and silent workers who believe that they can do nothing.

That is why the refusal of the Church under Fortich to remain silent caused such an uproar. It is easier now to understand why the Church is seen as enemy number one by certain people and why the bomb was thrown at Bishop Fortich.

Some years ago, while studying in Maryknoll, New York, I wrote a thesis entitled "Making a Choice between Revolutionary Counter-violence and Revolutionary Nonviolence on the Island of Negros." The title indicates a serious defect in the thesis: there is no mention of passivity. Most people in Negros do not choose revolutionary counter-violence or revolutionary nonviolence. *Most people in Negros choose passivity.* And in choosing passivity, they choose to continue the present system. Oppressors of large populations need collaborators—and indeed they always have them in ample number—but neither the oppressors nor the collaborators can do anything without the consent, without the silence, of you and me.

[5]

The Spurious Choice

In the long history of Negros basically only two alternatives have emerged in reacting to the unjust plantation system and the structures that keep it in place. One is armed struggle; the other is massive passivity. There are other alternatives, but historically they have found little room. The choice, the historic choice, has narrowed to resistance or submission, fight or flight. It is by restricting the alternatives to these two that the system in Negros has been able to continue so long. It is only when we extricate ourselves from the straitjacket of these limited alternatives that we will be able to open up to other possibilities.

Walter Wink is one of those who believes that this tyranny of false alternatives has been carefully nurtured by those who would hold on to power.

He says, for example, that the team of translators who translated the Bible for King James — the celebrated King James Version — deliberately chose words which would strengthen this assumption. He gives some examples:

When the court translators working in the hire of King James chose to translate *antistenai* as "Resist not evil," they were doing something more than rendering Greek into English. They were translating nonviolent resistance into docility. Jesus did not tell his oppressed hearers not to resist evil. That would have been absurd. His entire

79

ministry is utterly at odds with such a preposterous idea. The Greek word is made up of two parts: *anti,* a word still used in English meaning "against," and *histemi,* a verb which in its noun form (*stasis*) means violent rebellion, armed revolt, sharp dissension.

A proper translation of Jesus' teaching would then be, "Do not strike back at evil (or at one who has done you evil) in kind. Do not give blow for blow. Do not retaliate against violence with violence." Jesus was no less committed to opposing evil than the anti-Roman resistance fighters. The only difference was over the means to be used: how one should fight evil.

Now we are in a better position to see why King James' faithful servants translated *antistenai* as "resist not." The king would not want people concluding that they had any recourse against his or any other sovereign's unjust policies. *Therefore, the populace must be made to believe that there are two alternatives and only two: flight or fight.* Either we resist not or we resist. And Jesus commands us, according to these king's men, to resist not. Jesus appears to authorize monarchical absolutism. Submission is the will of God. Most modern translations have meekly followed in that path.[1]

But the proponents of fight or flight, resist or submit, go further. They present the famous "Turn the other cheek" passage as a counsel by Jesus to *submit*—and also the "Walk the other mile" and the "Give your cloak as well" passages. But such an interpretation makes submission into a Christian virtue, so that kings like James I and similar despotic monarchs have a free ride.

But another look at the "turn the other cheek" text shows that it means the exact opposite. The person slapped presents the other cheek and in so doing does not submit but challenges the aggressor *not* to hit him: "You have just done something despicable. You have hit an innocent person, but I know that you are better than your action betrays. I am giving you a second

chance, a chance to become the real you, a chance to be the human and dignified person you really are. I am willing to take the risk. Your refusal to hit me the second time will undo the first blow."

This is no submission; it is a daring challenge. It is what Hildegard and Jean Goss-Mayr call *"attaquant le coeur et la conscience"*[2] — attacking the heart and the conscience — the most vulnerable part of a human being because it is precisely that which makes us human.

The same is true for the other two passages: "If someone sues you in court for your shirt, let him have your coat as well" (Matt. 5:41). Someone is demanding you pay your debt by taking the shirt off your back (your undergarment) — right — give him your coat as well; stand naked before him, revealing the true nature of his evil. Picture the scene — that is no servile acceptance.

"If someone forces you to go one mile, go two miles with him" (Matt. 5:42). Jesus speaks to an audience of farmers who are vexed and oppressed by foreign troops. Their usual reaction is silent submission that harbors hatred and awaits revenge. He proposes something revolutionary. By Roman law a soldier could only ask a civilian to carry his burden for one mile — a wise Roman law to stop the soldiers from provoking revolts. Now Jesus proposes that the farmer spontaneously offer to walk another mile carrying the soldier's burden. The soldier is now in the wrong; the farmer has put him in a dilemma. If he accepts, he is in danger of being accused of breaking the law. The farmer has changed the whole dynamic of their relationship. The farmer is the one initiating the move; the soldier is the one reacting. All sorts of creative possibilities open up.

How far this is from the submission it has been used to bolster! The *Christian Community Bible* has a very good commentary on this:

> Those practicing Judo are taught how to put the adversary
> off balance: if he pushes you, you bring him towards you;
> if he pulls you forward, do not resist, but rather throw

yourself forward that he may fall down. Likewise, Jesus teaches us to give the opponent twice as much as he demands in order to disconcert his defenses, so that in the end he will realize he was mistaken.[3]

The crowds listening to Jesus must have chuckled. Suddenly they saw another way opening up — an alternative to submitting or fighting. Suddenly they were being told that submission is evil if it involves encouraging someone to do this to others. In this sort of submission we become accomplices in social injustice. Suddenly we are reminded that, yes, this is the enemy, but we must work to find a way not to eliminate him but to change him. This is truly a revolutionary way.

All of these are the opposite to passivity, and if we are ever in doubt about what Jesus meant in the New Testament, we should interpret his words in the light of his actions. When Jesus was struck, he did not submit passively. Though he was tied and in chains, as it were, and a prisoner, he immediately looked the servant of the high priest — the highest spiritual authority in the land — in the eye and said: "If I have spoken wrongly, point it out; but if I have spoken rightly, why do you strike me?" (John 18:23). If we are to take the meek and the mild interpretation of "if someone strikes you," then Jesus did not follow his own instructions. Restricting our reaction to injustice to the fight or submit alternatives has a long history. The breakthrough to other reactions is a historic development for the human species on a par in the evolutionary process with the breakthrough to intelligence. It will change the future of the race.

[6]

Active Nonviolence

Ten Unarmed Women

On a hill just outside the Muslim city of Marawi on the Island of Mindanao lives a group of ten Carmelite nuns. They have given their lives to prayer and chosen this spot to live in order to build peace and reconciliation between the two warring communities—Muslim and Christian.

The sisters were kidnapped en masse one night by some Muslim rebels and taken away to the surrounding mountains. After nine days of captivity and much ado they were finally released without the ransom this group of rebels hoped for.

Though the sisters were unscathed by the kidnapping, they knew that if it were to happen again, their presence there and their very vocation would be called into question by the Christians themselves. Some Christians had difficulty even with the concept of reconciliation and dialogue with the Muslims. The Philippine military suggested that the sisters keep guns, and for a while insisted on guarding them.

On September 4, 1987, at 5:30 in the morning, while it was still dark and the sisters were praying in the chapel, their convent was suddenly invaded by a dozen heavily armed Muslims in fatigue uniforms. The sisters pray Muslim style, sitting or kneeling on matting in a semicircle around the tabernacle. As the armed men surrounded them the sisters pulled closer

together and held hands and locked arms and began to pray the
Memorare:

> Remember O most gracious Virgin Mary that never was it
> known that anyone who fled to your protection implored
> your help, or sought your intercession was left unaided . . .

The armed men ordered them to come along, but the sisters
did not move. Sr. Ledesma from Negros was the prioress; she
realized that if they went along quietly nothing would happen
to them physically, but that another kidnapping would spell the
end of their mission of peace. She decided that they would not
go along even if it meant death.

At this stage the men were pulling at the sisters at the ends
of the semicircle; other men were going to the sisters in the
middle and pushing grenades at their faces and starting to count.
One burly rebel leveled a machine gun at them and released the
safety catch with an ominous crack. The sisters pulled even
closer together, the tears streaming down their faces. Sr.
Ledesma said: "Hold on. Our Lady is with us." At that moment
each sister had decided in her heart that she was ready to die.
As one said to me: "This would be our last Mass; we would die
right there at the altar."

Through their tears many of the sisters managed to look at
the men, and one of the sisters said, "You are *good* people."
Another said: "We have been praying for you." At these words
the men lowered their heads.

The next forty minutes, "the longest forty minutes in our
lives," was an extraordinary tug of war: These armed men, tug-
ging at the frail women locked together on their knees; the men
wilting under the pressure of the tears, the prayers, the determination of the women and themselves gradually being filled
with a rising sense of shame.

Suddenly the sound of a car arriving was heard. It was the
priest arriving for Mass. Well, actually he had arrived a few
minutes before, realized from the sounds what had happened
and was rushing away for help. The men had had enough; they

fled. Some of them had ransacked the house but found almost nothing—a ballpoint pen, some grocery money.

Later, when the Philippine Army military commander was interviewing the sisters he said, "From what I've heard I can assure you, sisters, these men will never return." No more words about the need for guns.

Ten unarmed women had overcome twelve heavily armed men. They not only defeated them but probably touched their hearts so that they left that convent different from when they came in.

When we think of nonviolence today, certain images come to mind. We think of Mahatma Gandhi and his great campaigns across India against the caste system, which barred the untouchables from so many walks of life; his civil disobedience to unjust laws of the Raj—the British colonial government; his *Satyagraha* or truth force; his program for an alternative society; his public fast against the internecine strife between Muslims and Hindus. His assassination.

We think of the now almost legendary exploits of Martin Luther King, Jr. We remember the refusal of Rosa Parks to give up her seat in the bus and stand so that a white man could sit when she was ordered to do so by the bus conductor, and the subsequent strike by the black people of Montgomery, Alabama.

We think of the great civil rights campaigns across the Southern states, and that historic moment in Birmingham, Alabama, when a group of unarmed blacks, marching to a prayer meeting, were confronted by police dogs and high-powered hoses, hoses that could take the bark off a tree. Commissioner "Bull" Conner ordered the hoses turned on. But the blacks kept coming and Bull's own police disobeyed him and stepped back. That was a moment! And then King's "I've been to the mountaintop" speech the night before he was murdered.

We think of the Vietnam war resistance and groups like the Plowshares, the Catonsville Nine. We consider Fr. Dan Berrigan, or later Brian Willson in California lying across the railway tracks to stop the train from the Concord Naval Station carrying weapons for Central America. That train did not stop.

In France they think of Shantidas—the French Gandhi with his communities of The Arc and their long resistance to militarization of the French farming countryside.

In New Zealand and Australia they think of the courageous crew of Greenpeace sailing into France's nuclear testing zone.

In Austria they think of Franz Jaggerstatter, the peasant farmer who withstood the Nazis to their face and chose to be executed rather than join in Hitler's war.

In Czechoslovakia they think of Jan Palach, the student who in 1969 burned himself to death in protest at the Russian occupation. Half a million mourners attended his funeral. The Russians had to guard his grave for years; that grave was subversive.

And of course in talking of nonviolence we think of the heroic refusal of peace people like the Mennonites and Quakers to take up arms.

In the Philippines to talk of nonviolence is to call up images of the February revolt in 1986 when people kneeling in the streets stopped Marcos's tanks.

More recently still, and in some way inspired by the Manila events, we saw the massive crowds of civilians in Berlin and Leipzig and Prague with their candlelight processions bringing down those forty-year-old despotic regimes.

And then more poignantly, a scene which brought tears to my eyes, that lone boy cycling up to the row of tanks advancing through Tiananmen Square. The first tank slows, and he abandons his bike and stands right in front of that tank with waving arms. Then, when the tank and the succeeding file of tanks have halted, he clambers up on the tank and remonstrates with the driver. We could only see his gesticulations, we could not hear his voice. But I could "hear" it. He was saying, "We're your brothers—why are doing this to us?" No one has ever found out the young man's name or who he was; perhaps it is better that way for he now represents every man and woman and child in the world who believes that war is folly.

Such are the images, some heroic, that come to mind when we think of active nonviolence. But we need to boil them down and extract the essence of what nonviolence is. We need a working definition.

What Active Nonviolence Is Not

However, before we examine in detail what active nonviolence is, we have to look carefully at what it is not. This is necessary because otherwise we will not understand why some people who have dedicated their lives to working for justice dislike and distrust active nonviolence. It may be clear why dictators don't like active nonviolence, but why should people who work for justice feel distrustful of it?

It is also necessary to say clearly what nonviolence is not because in some places, like Negros, prominent government people and even military people continuously use the word nonviolence while still holding firmly to a military solution to the problems of Negros. In these cases the word is used to befuddle the public. If you believe in the just-war theory, then say so, no one will despise you; it is after all the majority opinion. But don't try to have it both ways. There is a grace in naming things correctly; indeed no change can come until we do. So a few words on what is *not* nonviolence.

Nonviolence is not neutrality. In Negros people grasp at the word *nonviolence* like a drowning person grasps at a plank. Again and again people say, "I am neutral; I am for nonviolence." But that is a contradiction. Neutrality is a vote for the status quo, and the status quo in Negros is very violent.

Nonviolence is not a dramatic or romantic deus ex machina, a magic wand waved to undo the evil of centuries without the pain of altering and building new social structures. True, there have been moments in history when that essential godliness of human beings has burst through and nonviolence has brought about dramatic and beautiful changes. Such actions can change the course of history, and they also perform the important function of building up the myth (in the positive sociological sense) of nonviolence. But usually change is not dramatic.

Nonviolence is not cowardice. To take up arms against an unjust cause means putting one's life in danger. It demands a certain amount of bravery. Some have the idea that nonviolence is the cowardly option. Not so. The decision to get involved in nonviolence demands bravery because one's life is all the more in danger as a result. Thousands of people have been killed in the Philippines as a result of being involved in active nonviolence; for example, the massacre at Escalante, Negros Occidental, in September 1985 when the Civilian Home Defense Force shot into an unarmed crowd. Those who went to that peaceful demonstration in that very violent town knew the administration had a history of violence. They were aware that they were in danger, but they went ahead. Gandhi had something to say on this matter:

> Nonviolence and cowardice go ill together. I can imagine a fully armed man to be at heart a coward. Possession of arms implies an element of fear, if not cowardice. But true nonviolence is an impossibility without the possession of unadulterated fearlessness.

And again:

> My creed of nonviolence is an extremely active force. It has no room for cowardice or even weakness. There is hope for a violent man to be, some day, nonviolent. But, there is none for a coward.[1]

In *Revolution from the Heart* I tell the story of my friend Renato, who wanted to join the revolutionaries. He consulted me. I disagreed, but left the choice to him. He did not join but worked with a priest in the lowlands in an Education for Justice program. The local barrio captain, opposed to all this justice work, ordered Renato killed, and he was stabbed to death by the barrio militia. When Renato was dying, he told those around him that he was happy that he had given his life in this way.[2] When we take up the way of nonviolence we promise not to use violence on others, but there is no guarantee that we ourselves will not suffer violence.

I have dwelt on this point of cowardice because it frequently happens that young people ask themselves, "Am I brave enough to put my life in danger and take up arms and join the revolution?" This can be a mischievous question appealing to their self-image. It also subtly implies that real bravery is only there when people hold a gun in their hand. It can cloud the real issue, which is "Is taking up arms the most effective remedy for this situation?" Is taking up arms right?

Nonviolence is not an end in itself; it is a means. The end purpose is life with justice, the beginnings, the "already but not yet" of the Kingdom of God. It is precisely this lack of justice that lays the basis for violence. If we want to remove violence we must first remove injustice.

Many people ignore the truth that the root of violence is injustice; they want to stop the violence, but they are not particularly interested in removing the injustice — the word *nonviolence* is always on their lips. Walter Wink, in the context of the apartheid conflict in South Africa, illustrates this point:

> Many whites have developed a sudden new interest in having blacks become nonviolent and that too must be read as a cynical attempt to avoid the consequences of an unjust system rather than an attempt to address its root causes. Most Christians desire nonviolence, yes, but they are not talking about nonviolent struggle for justice. They mean simply the absence of conflict. They would like the system to change without having to be involved in changing it. What they mean by nonviolence is as far from nonviolent direct action as a lazy nap in the sun is from confrontation in which protesters are being clubbed to the ground.[3]

The task, then, for those who would eradicate violence, is one of a long struggle against injustice in all its forms. That is why the Church has continually linked peace and justice. Pius XII's motto was: *Opus Iustitiae Pax* — "Peace is the result of working for justice."

It is important to say what nonviolence is *not* because some people who are working for justice become justifiably angry at seeing the word and the concept used as a smokescreen to stop legitimate action for justice. One recalls Chief Butalezi's intervention against sanctions in South Africa—a classic nonviolent tactic—"I am against sanctions, I am for nonviolence!" A contradiction.

In the Philippines this anger is particularly apparent because so often the advice to use nonviolence is perceived to be coming from people in the United States. In the light of recent Philippine history that appears to many as ironic.

Why is it we always seem to hear the question of nonviolence from Americans? Americans, who barged in and stole our country from us just when we succeeded in kicking out the Spanish colonialists! Americans who, to keep a grip on their new colony, slaughtered hundreds of thousands of Filipinos at the beginning of the century! Americans, who incinerated women and children in the villages of Vietnam with napalm! Americans, who maintain an economic world order to over-fatten the rich in their own country. Americans, who maintain on our soil two of the largest military bases outside the U.S. in order to perpetuate this system of injustice and institutionalized violence . . . and now, it is Americans who come and ask us why we are violent.[4]

Feelings run high because the word *nonviolence* is often appropriated by very violent people and distorted for their purposes.

However that may be, in the long struggle for peace based on justice we need to be the ones who have the patience and discernment to see through such distortion. We should not allow ourselves to be robbed of a precious thing because there are those who abuse it, neglect it, manipulate it.

A Working Description of Active Nonviolence

Nonviolence is based on the principle of the inviolability of the human person. It calls for a life of action; assertive, imaginative, systemic, preemptive action. This action is aimed at uprooting injustice and eventually bringing about reconciliation. At times when the evil is upon us nonviolence may call for courageous and faith-filled sacrifice. In all of this, nonviolence uses only those means that are in conformity with its ends. Further, for Christian disciples these actions are inspired in a special way by the life of Jesus and by Jesus alive.

Inviolability: Inviolability of the human person is absolute and must be understood within the context of the integrity of all creation. Jean Goss-Mayr put it this way: "The human being is to be respected in an absolute manner and without exception. All other values must serve human life but in return human beings have the responsibility to safeguard the environment and world resources."[5]

Assertive Action: Nonviolence is not something you *don't* do; rather, it is a whole program of assertive actions to which you dedicate your life. However, it has been dogged by a problem of language since the beginning. Gandhi faced this when he invented the word *satyagraha.* The first word he had been using was *ahimsa*, which means "no harm." *Satyagraha* literally means "Adherence to the Truth." It could be translated as, that force that comes from doing the truth; thus it becomes a positive concept, something you do rather than something you avoid.

In the English language an early word in vogue was *pacifism*, but that obviously has connotations of doing nothing—and unfortunately sounds very like *passivism*—so many prefer the word *nonviolence.* To counteract the negative prefix *non*, the word *active* was added. Now it is common in the Philippines to abbreviate it simply to ANV. I myself at times prefer the term *revolutionary nonviolence*, because it makes it quite clear that we are aiming at a total renewal and transformation of society. But no matter what we call it, those who are involved know that while at times it may involve patience, most times it involves a very high level of positive activity.

Imaginative: The powers of the imagination have been very neglected. Our imagination is like an unexplored continent. In nonviolent action we are forced to explore it. The point is well explained by Sr. Madonna Kolbenschlag in a talk she gave on feminist spirituality. She sees the imaginative response to be so different from the conventional response that it is of an altogether different order, of a "second order."

> To believe in the possibility of change demands imagination. It is to believe in surprising systems by introducing creative, imaginative, unexpected responses to the same old problems. Genuine change most often occurs through a "second order" response: one which rethinks the solution previously tried, and suggests a solution altogether unexpected.
>
> The quality of paradox and surprise is at the heart of "second order" change. It requires a radical breaking out of the framework and conceptual blocks that limit our imagination. That is why "second order" change occurs so often in impasse situations. In a genuine impasse, every normal way of action is brought to a standstill. The left side of the brain, with its usual application of conventional thinking, grinds to a halt. The impasse drives us back to contemplation, forces the right brain into gear, seeking intuitive unconventional answers to the situation. It is very close to revelation![6]

Borrowing a Jewish proverb, which came from the Polish concentration camps, she sums up her point: "When faced with two alternatives, always choose the third."

Gandhi was a master of the imaginative response. Take his long march to the sea to make salt in 1930. The British in India had a monopoly on salt, which they taxed heavily. Gandhi saw that not only was the tax unjust and oppressive to the poor, but the money gained from it bolstered the British government. He conceived of a plan to undo the injustice, remove the support and at the same time perform an act of civil disobedience — making salt. The action was nonviolent in character, but magnificently symbolic of what could be done if everyone united.

He announced his intention to make salt but said he was first

going to make the twenty-day journey on foot to the sea, to the beach at Dandi. And as he walked along barefoot and wearing the clothes of the lowest caste of peasant, he stopped and explained to the people what he was going to do and why he was going to do it.

As he went, the world watched through the newspapers and the crowds walking with him grew. By the time he reached the sea, millions of Indians were willing to take the risk of making salt themselves, and the British rule was seen to be fallible and vulnerable. The emperor was wearing no clothes at all. A major step had been made on the Indian nonviolent road to freedom.

A group here in Negros was giving a seminar on development to a mixed group of *hacenderos* and laborers. One of the exercises was to play a game in which the participants had to imagine what they would do if they won a million pesos and could spend it as they wished. It was pathetic to hear the laborers explaining what they would do with it; with the imaginary million pesos few of them managed to get even as far as the city of Bacolod on the island of Negros. The imagination, someone has said, is the deepest prison of all. That surely means that even if we had all the means of removing oppression and injustice at our disposal but did not have the imagination to realize it or put them together in a constructive way, then we could not move. We would be like the little eagle in the fable, who was adopted as a fledgling by the ducks. He grew up with the ducks, thought he was a duck and used to look up at the birds flying overhead and think it would be nice to join them. But he never did. He was a duck.

Systemic Actions: Injustice has been institutionalized; so must nonviolence be. It must be carefully planned, flexible, long-term, programmed and built into the structure of life. To achieve this, nonviolence must be a permanent constituent of society, built into religion, education, law and culture. It must be part of the system. Today it rarely is. On the contrary, violence is built into the system of our present worldwide society right down to the toys we train our children with.

In Philippine high schools and colleges up and down the

nation a form of youth military service is obligatory. We are treated to the spectacle of boys and girls from the age of thirteen up to the end of college parading in military uniforms with imitation guns and learning military jargon and tactics. Nothing could be more calculated to prepare people mentally for the idea that the gun is the solution to problems of the Philippines.

It is possible to institutionalize nonviolence so as to make it a viable defense plan for a nation. Gene Sharp, who runs the Center for Nonviolent Action at Harvard, has given his life to these studies. In his book *Making Europe Unconquerable* (without an army!) he develops the whole idea and strategy of nonviolent defense on a notion known as civilian-based defense.[7] He shows how, if civilian-based defense is institutionalized by a nation, the people will be able to deprive any invading country of the fruits of invasion and therefore make their invasion not worthwhile. Hence, it acts as a powerful deterrent.

But Gandhi made it clear that if we are planning to do away with one way of life we should also be planning for an alternative to take its place. We should have what Gandhi called his constructive program. We can't have a vacuum. We should be planning now and already introducing bit by bit an alternative program. I like the expression often quoted by Dorothy Day — "building the new world within the shell of the old." Now is the time to be developing small farming co-ops in Negros, which can eventually spread down and take the place of the plantations.

The court system is one systemic nonviolent way for getting redress of injuries and injustice. But on Negros there is no way the poor can afford legal assistance. Bishop Fortich started a free legal aid office, which gave access to honest lawyers for the very poor anywhere in the Diocese of Bacolod in criminal cases. To save the poor from the expensive journey to Bacolod, attorneys Frankie Cruz, Romeo Subaldo, Archi Baribar and Johnny Hagad made regular visits to the southern town of Kabankalan to hold special office just for them. Thus a classic nonviolent service was institutionalized.

Preemptive Actions: Like good health care, nonviolence at its best is preventive rather than curative; it is not a fire engine called in to quell the flames. To wait till a situation of injustice has developed into a conflagration and then propose nonviolence is to court failure. Nonviolence is not a magic solution, though it most certainly does have a mystical and spiritual dimension, particularly in its "reactive" form. It is preemptive action based on cold calculating analysis of the past, and shrewd prognosis of the future. Hitler realized the necessity of preemption when he laid the basis for the power that allowed him to carry out his violence, his "final solution" on the Jews. Long before he became chancellor he said:

> We must not imagine that one could suddenly take out of a briefcase the drafts of a new State constitution and impose them dictatorially on the state of command . . . by a decree of power from above.[8]

Nonviolence has to be as foresighted as Hitler was. But the children of this world are sometimes wiser in their generation than the children of light. In fact, if we were to apply preemptive nonviolence to the extermination of the Jews, we would have to begin back in the 1850s in Germany when the "superior race" theories became popular. At that stage a courageous Church, true to gospel values, would have condemned those theories severely as being contrary to the heart of the gospel message. Or again in Vienna, a Catholic city, at the turn of the century, when the adolescent mind of Hitler was being formed, a courageous and faithful Church would have opposed the virulent anti-Semitism, which was publicly proclaimed and had such an influence on the young Hitler.

It is the aim of preemptive nonviolence to make sure that these evils are stillborn, precisely because it (preemptive non-violence) aborts them before their birth and, preferably, works to see that they will never be conceived.

But when things have been let go too far, active nonviolence is still not helpless. There are well-documented cases where people stood up to Hitler's demonic steamroller and actually succeeded. In Denmark, where the Danes refused to hand over the Jews, almost no Jews were killed.[9] There is also the case, mentioned earlier, of the Norwegian school teachers who in 1942 refused to teach Nazism in the schools and eventually forced Minister-President Vidkun Quisling to relent. There is the case of the Jews in Sofia, Bulgaria, in May 1943. An agreement for the deportation of the first batch of twenty thousand Jews to the East German Territories and to their death was signed. Floods of letters and telegrams were sent to Parliament; the people and the Jews themselves protested. The Gentiles mingled with the Jews, who marched in an impressive protest. The authorities backed down and did not carry out the deportation of the Jews. The Jews of Bulgaria were saved.[10]

And there is the lesser known but now carefully documented case where several thousand Jewish husbands were released in Germany itself in 1943 when their Gentile wives came screaming and crying outside the places of detention. All were released.[11]

A Philippine example of preemptive nonviolence is the civilian poll watch during the snap election of 1986. Fortich was vice-chairman. The watchers were heroic, used classic nonviolent procedure and were effective. The tragedy is that they seem to have evaporated now that the magnetic drawing force of the anti-Marcos movement is gone. But without a brave independent civilian poll watch, trained in nonviolent tactics, we cannot hope to have social transformation through elections in Negros or the Philippines.

A more enduring example is the one of Midsilip. For years the people of Midsilip, a town on the Island of Mindanao south of Negros, had been trying to stop the logging which was destroying their forests. Once the hills were logged over, the rivers dried up, flash floods hit whole areas, the nesting grounds of the fish were smothered in fluvial mud, irrigation systems were destroyed and the land eroded.

Ten years of protest to the government (1976-87) only resulted in the reply: "We have the case under study." In May 1987 seven hundred responsible citizens sent a letter to the minister of the environment and ten days later made a *Fiesta sa Kinaiyahan,* a special religious feast and procession to celebrate creation, God's grace through the earth. On June 12 they held the first people's picket to stop the logging. The picketers said, "Sell what you've cut but stop cutting." However, the trucks loaded with logs rolled on day and night. Then the citizens filed a case in court, that brought the chief of the Forestry Division, Mr. Loreto Ordiz, to the scene. He promised results, but none came. The legal efforts went on and on till Fr. Frank Nally, a Columban priest from Ireland, one Sunday at Mass challenged the people to act. The people now initiated a permanent People Power Picket. Starting with Mass, the people from all the surrounding Christian Communities blocked the routes of the log-carrying trucks day and night. They aimed to force the government to cancel the logging concession. But, still no cancellation.

On and on. Reading the record of the case is emotionally exhausting; it recounts how the logging companies, the military and the government combined in every sort of deception to continue the logging, including the setting up of anti-communist vigilantes. Death threats followed. But the day and night picket of the people continued till the whole diocese was involved. Warrants of arrest were issued for seven picketers, including Fr. Nally. Three soldiers were killed near the picket line in inter-military rivalry. Finally, after four months of picketing day and night, Minister Factoran ordered the cancellation of the license of the Sunville Logging Company. Then, in a last fling of retaliation, the vigilantes lined up the picketers and threatened to shoot them if they ran or even moved. They said they would kill Fr. Nally, and they took away the logs impounded by the picketers. However, the picketers had won the day; the logging concession was canceled. This is a marvelous example of brave reactive nonviolence in the face of danger. Preemptive nonviolence stopped the destruction of the livelihood of thousands of people, which would have led to untold violence at some future date.

Here was a case of active and reactive nonviolence working together harmoniously to create a powerful effect. The idea of nonviolently blockading trucks carrying illegal logs from forests has spread all over the Philippines.[12]

Aimed at Uprooting Injustice: The immediate target of nonviolent action is not violence but injustice. The old dictum that violence begets violence is very misleading because it presumes that the first violence comes from nowhere. The dictum would better read: Injustice begets violence, and that violence begets counter-violence.

Another well-known phrase used frequently when referring to people involved in acts of violence is *mindless violence.* True, there is such a thing as mindless violence; for example, when a person runs amok or as a result of certain natural phenomena. But most of the violence we meet in the world has its origin in a sane mind, and no matter how horrific the acts of so-called terrorists, they are not normally mindless. Rather, the mind has played a very great part. The mind has decided to retaliate against acts of perceived injustice, usually because no other way of "getting even" is available. In the international debate which followed the United States bombing of Libya in April 1986, many observers concluded that the essential mistake the State Department made was presuming that the acts of terrorism took place because the perpetrators were evil and not because, basically, the Palestinians had no homeland. These observers remarked that the terrorism would only go away when its ultimate cause, Palestinian homelessness, was dealt with. Meanwhile, the United States was dealing with the symptoms not with the causes. We pay a heavy price for not naming things correctly.[13]

A Way of Life: Nonviolence should be part of a *way of life*, not just unrelated acts added to our life. Nonviolence should be part of our way of life. We need to move toward a personal simplicity of lifestyle. We need to live lightly on the earth, mindful of the limitation of the earth's resources.

But of what use is a personally abstemious lifestyle if the work we do itself reinforces the overall structures of injustice? Take, for example, a sincere and practicing Christian, working honestly in the World Bank to process a loan for a lumber company or a power station which will destroy the basis of life of a whole tribe. It happens all the time. Such a person's asceticism is a mockery because the consequences of his or her daily work is the destruction of others.

A relative of mine, possibly influenced by hearing stories from me about conditions in the Philippines and the Third World generally, proposed to give up his job and uproot himself and join the Asian Development Bank. Just at that time that bank had financed the infrastructure — roads and bridges — to facilitate a new sugar mill opening on the Island of Mindanao in the southern Philippines. But that mill was actively putting small farmers off the surrounding land and turning independent people into dependent peons, locked into the same old treadmill. Some might conceivably have a small rise in income; all would be ultimately gravely diminished in spirit. I advised him strongly against joining the bank.

We must examine our position in the complex hierarchy of structures and see if by our work or avocation, we are strengthening the destructive forces or helping to transform them. Are we in fact part of the problem? If we are, how can we change to become part of the overall undoing of the problem. As we struggle toward integrating our lifestyle and our way of life, we become truly nonviolent.

Bringing About Reconciliation: Reconciliation is the ultimate aim of nonviolence because nonviolence holds not only for the absolute inviolability of the human person, both friend and enemy, but maintains that human beings are ultimately one family, brothers and sisters to each other. Hence, it is important that active nonviolence use a style and methodology that does not contradict this end and does not close the door to eventual reconciliation. However, because reconciliation is an ultimate (not an immediate) goal and because the word *reconciliation* has been sorely abused and manipulated, it will need a special chapter of its own.

Means and Ends: It is a central tenet of active nonviolence that the means it uses should not contradict its ultimate goal. Hence, taking life is always out. Evil is not to be located in the person but in the structure. Removing the person does not remove the evil. Too often, those who with noble intent have sought to liquidate oppressors have found themselves using the same means to deal with disagreements within their own ranks. Having guillotined the king and queen, Robespierre then guillotined his own companions; then he was guillotined himself by those who remained.

For those struggling against oppression the attraction of the gun always remains. I used to say to our co-workers: "If your enemy is good at checkers and you are good at chess, why agree to play checkers with him?" The military like the game of guns because for any guns we can get, they can get bigger guns, and if we get bigger guns, they get helicopter gunships and mortars. Whoever thought we'd see tanks in Negros? — and yet we have them now! But when it comes to truth and conscience, that's where they are weakest. Consequently, that should be our forte, attacking the heart and the conscience.

In the ongoing dialogue over using or not using weapons some people insistently put forward arguments that envision someone coming at us with a gun. There is frequently an assumption that the intended victim already holds a weapon and now has to decide whether to use it or not. This already limits the options to kill or be killed. But people who have previously made a decision for nonviolence will most probably *not* have a weapon, so their mind is freed for other creative alternatives — is *forced* to other creative alternatives.

Another assumption in these questions is that being killed is the ultimate evil. For the believer in nonviolence, killing itself is the ultimate evil.

I must confess here that on that occasion when a thousand people from my parish were mobilized for nonviolent action, two of our members carried large farm knives. I disagreed, but I was in a minority and had to agree to that compromise. The knives played no part, other than reassurance, but I regret now that I didn't take a stronger stand. We don't become nonviolent overnight; it's a journey, and sometimes we have to ask God's forgiveness and try again.

Practitioners of active nonviolence differ when it comes to inflicting light physical injury. Gandhi for a while held to a scrupulous extreme whereby he did not want his wife even to have an injection. For my part, I have no problem in accepting karate style self-defense used in the spirit of nonviolence. On one occasion when they were working in Brazil, Jean and Hildegard Goss-Mayr were suddenly confronted by a man threatening them with a knife. Jean gave the man a karate chop on the wrist — the knife dropped to the ground. Jean snatched it away and then spent a long time talking to the man, who regretted his act and poured out the cause of his frustration.

For a Christian: We tread carefully here because Christians have no monopoly on nonviolence. Indeed, the greatest practitioner of nonviolence of the twentieth century, Mohandas Gandhi, was a devout Hindu. However, he was inspired by Christ; his problem with Christianity was that Christians weren't following Christ in this matter. But for a Christian, Jesus is the model. He absorbed evil without retaliating *in kind*. For Christ, life was more sacred even than the holiest law of the Sabbath. "This is the truth of God in history. As the deepest truth of the universe it is the only way forward."[14]

Jesus Alive: For a Christian, it is not just a question of Christ's teaching and example, however. There is more. There is the mystery: Christ is alive and *with us* on this impossible journey, making it possible.

Two Modes of Active Nonviolence

If we glance through the preceding examples of active nonviolence, we will notice that some of them are cases where we work to prevent the injustice that gives rise to the future violence while others are cases where the situation has deteriorated already into open conflict.

I call this latter type of nonviolence *reactive nonviolence*, because people are forced to react now to a present and immediate threat; the war is on, destruction is imminent and the believer, armed with only faith, responds to the situation, stands up before the evil machine of violence and is ready to die. It is too late to take preventive steps. This type of nonviolence could be described as a heroic act of faith in humankind and in the elemental goodness that we believe resides in every person. If the "enemy" can be contacted in person, then this act of faith and trust by the believer may even affect the "enemy" by "attacking the heart and the conscience" and so turn them back.

But, if not, the believer holds that his or her life has still not been wasted. It has been offered up on the altar of a greater truth; namely, that it is better to be killed than to kill. To destroy another is ultimately to destroy oneself, and to give up one's life for this truth is ultimately to build up the whole human family. Even if such a heroic act is never seen by human eye, it is recorded in the heart of the world; no act of that order is ever lost.

This type of nonviolence tends to emphasize the heroism of nonviolent action, the rightness and sacredness of nonviolent action rather than the effectiveness.

But nonviolent action *is* effective. And it will be more effective precisely in the degree to which it is *preemptive* and does not wait for the situation to deteriorate. We are not always given the luxury of knowing beforehand that this particular situation will deteriorate if not dealt with now. Nonetheless, our present-day experience may help us recognize classic situations that, if allowed to develop, will become so critical that only heroic action can deal with them. Some examples of preemptive nonviolence follow.

Work for Democracy: Participation by the citizenry in the decisions made about them is insurance against widespread injustice. So, work for genuine democracy will always be opposed in countries where it is lacking. This is an obvious field for those who wish to be involved in nonviolent action. A friend of mine used to say to me: "Niall, it's OK to talk of nonviolent action in India. The British had a democratic tradition. They didn't just mow people down. But here in the Philippines it's not possible." He was wrong. It is precisely where brutal dictatorships are in power that the nonviolent methods are necessary. Otherwise, whole populations face genocide. (And at times the British did mow people down in India: *Amritsar*.)

Work for Land Reform: Democracy is hollow where large land-holders control the votes of the people on their land. Bishop Fortich once said to me that the reason some people in Negros oppose land reform so much is because as long as they could "deliver" a certain number of votes, they had a say in who would be mayor, and once they had the mayor in their debt then they had a say in who would be governor, and so on.

Apart from that, lack of land, dispossession, a toiling and oppressed peasantry is a tinder box for violent revolution. The long haul of work to bring about land reform is classic, nonviolent action. In Ireland, when the ex-revolutionary Michael Davitt joined landlord Charles Stewart Parnell in initiating the now historic Land League, both crossed an ideological line to join in a nonviolent campaign to bring about the most profound of all Ireland's revolutions: the return of the land to the people. But the land campaign took from 1870 till the Wyndham Land Act of 1903 to succeed. And Charles Stewart Parnell was destroyed in the process. My grandmother used to tell me how, when she was a little girl, Parnell arrived at their village in Waterford in 1888. A widow and her family were to be evicted by the landlord from her home for not being able to pay the rent; the house would then be put to the torch. Parnell had all the children brought from the school to watch this harrowing event. The weeping woman was turned out of her house and her bits of furniture piled up outside. The constabulary—Irish men all and probably from the same background as the woman—were humiliated by the presence of the now crying school children—maybe some were their own children. At the last moment, as the thatch was about to be set alight, Parnell and the local Land League Committee stepped forward and paid the overdue rent. The woman was saved and the tears were dried. At least one little girl never forgot that day, which was exactly as Parnell and Davitt had intended in their campaign to erode consent to the landlord system.

Gandhi himself, studying in London at the time, followed the events surrounding Parnell and the struggle for land reform. His followers had made land reform a basic plank in the nonviolent movement. Indeed, it is highly probable that Gandhi's use of the boycott was influenced by the Irish example.[15]

In Negros, Violeta Lopez-Gonzaga has dedicated herself to the land reform question. She has done vital research on land reform and published it under titles such as *The Sacadas: A Poverty Profile; Crisis and Poverty in Sugarlandia;* and *The Socio-Politics of Sugar.* She has also gone into the field and followed up specific cases. As a result she has received death threats and court summonses. Apart from that, her books have earned her the title of communist. But the work she is doing is essential if land reform is ever to take place. It is preemptive nonviolence at its best.

Work for Human Rights: The more oppressive a regime is, the more it needs to violate humans rights to keep the people in line. Monitoring and reporting human rights violations is nonviolent action and calls at times for great courage.

Work for Civil Rights: When parts of the population do not have full civil rights, for example, under apartheid in South Africa, then violence is in the offing. To work for civil rights is active nonviolence; in fact, it was the civil rights campaigns in the United States and India that helped active nonviolence develop as a political philosophy.

Work for the Rule of Law and Fair Courts: When we were interned in the Negros provincial jail, we did a survey on the nature of the cases of the other prisoners (the two hundred prisoners in the high security section with us). Almost all were in for murder, but the amazing thing was that most of those murders were revenge killings or perceived self-defense killings. Where was the law? Many prisoners were in for years and years without their cases being tried. One man was in for eleven years. Three of his children had died while he was in prison, and when the case finally was judged (after eleven years and much pushing from us), it was dismissed. Reform of the judicial and legal system is a priority for nonviolent action.

Looking back at the examples you can see that the first list involves nonviolent action in the midst of the fray, so to speak, while the second list exemplifies preemptive nonviolent action to uproot the causes of violence. Both aspects are necessary according to the times and situations that prevail and both types work together to reinforce each other. At times they telescope into each other and become almost indistinguishable.

Gandhi: The Classic Practitioner of Nonviolence

Mohandas Gandhi (1869-1948) combined preemptive and reactive nonviolence in one great effective symphony which restored dignity to the Indians in South Africa and ultimately expelled the British from the Indian subcontinent — without the shedding of blood.

Gandhi's vision began in poor rural villages where he emphasized self-reliance and village-based industries. His revival of the spinning wheel both developed village self-reliance and undermined external colonial control. As he made his endless pilgrimages on foot throughout the villages he highlighted the beauty and simplicity of the peasant lifestyle and drew from their own religious sources the energy and grace to overcome communal violence and injustice and the scandal of the caste system, especially as it affected the untouchables. His was an integrated approach to peace; as he attacked the old structure he tried to build the new.

On September 24, 1948, at New Delhi, Mohandas Gandhi was shot to death while he was on a religious fast to bring about reconciliation between Muslims and Christians. Thus he became the example for his own teaching that nonviolence is not the easy option.

It is tragic and significant that Gandhi is unknown in Negros and the Philippines except for the more dramatic images from his life. Yet he is the sage for our times. The discovery of his vision and the secret of his success must be part of any serious attempt to transform society in Negros and the Third World.

[7]

Does It Work?

Effectiveness Versus Rightness

My own awakening to nonviolence was gradual. It came first from a gut feeling that no matter how clear the arguments in favor of killing they did not seem to sit easily with my understanding of Jesus Christ and his willingness to die for those who were killing him. Would he have killed in just self-defense? In fact, the case did arise. He was offered swords to defend himself, and he chided those who offered them and prayed for his executioners (Lk. 22:49–51; Matt. 26:51–54).

For the individual disciple, it seemed to me, killing must be unacceptable. But that made me deeply uneasy. Was I going down the road of total impracticality? Fine to do it oneself, but could one invite others down that road? The case was put to me when the young man Nato, who had been a member of a farmers' co-op I had started, came to me one night and said simply, "I'm going to join the New Peoples Army." He said that he was going to kill Sergeant Rosano, a man who had killed some fifty people and recently had been implicated in the torture of Vilma, one of our catechists. I looked at him for a long time and then said, "I do not believe that is the way to right this wrong." Then I took down my copy of *Populorum Progressio*, which we had translated into Ilonggo, and I read him paragraph 31, which gives the conditions for a just revolution. I closed the book and said, "You know your rights; according to the Church's teaching the time can come for a person to take up arms. As for myself, I'm not too sure that I agree with the teaching of the Church in this matter!" Before he left he said, "It's not that I want to take a life. I want to save lives; by killing Rosano I would save lives." We parted.[1]

As it turned out, the NPA did not accept him. Instead he took up the nonviolent approach working with a Filipino priest's conscientization program, and he was eventually killed on the orders of the local barrio captain. I was convinced at this stage that active nonviolence was right, but I had no evidence yet that it worked. It was about this time that I came across the three volumes of Gene Sharp's *The Politics of Nonviolent Action.*

Gene Sharp has spent a lifetime examining the practicality, the effectiveness (as distinct from the rightness) of active nonviolence. He has attempted to document the successes and failures of active nonviolence since the beginning of recorded history.

A look through the headings of some of the eight hundred sections of Sharp's three volumes showed me just how little I really knew of active nonviolence. Sharp's argument is that given the proper preparation, with all that that implies, and other things being equal, active nonviolence beats violence hands down on effectiveness in the long run. However, active nonviolence, he insists, doesn't work without putting in the necessary mental energy, the study, the preparation, the training, the practice, the creative imagination and the sacrifice to at least the same extent as is necessary for successful armed struggle. Where would armed struggle be without its training, tactics and strategies?

Regarding effectiveness, Sharp cites Jawaharlal Nehru, the man who eventually led India to independence; Nehru did not believe in nonviolence as an ethic for life or as a religious imperative. However, he did support Gandhi's nonviolent way of expelling the British from India. And he has given his reasons in his autobiography, *Towards Freedom*:

We had accepted that method (Satyagraha), the Congress has made that method its own because of *a belief in its effectiveness*. Gandiji had placed it before the country not only as the right method but as the most effective one for our purpose (emphasis added).[2]

I am now personally convinced that active nonviolence in the long run is more effective than counter-violence, and I recommend that anyone who feels active nonviolence is utopian take the trouble to go through those volumes by Sharp. They open an amazing and exciting world of possibilities.

In the village of Oringao outside the town of Kabankalan in Southern Negros in the early 1980s, a landowner of means had illegally and immorally taken over the small wet rice field of a sharecropper. The sharecropper's name was Juanito Serrantes. This landowner, Ramon Sanito, had the power that comes with education, family—his relatives owned surrounding lands—and a close connection with the military. In particular he had engaged the services of Sgt. Rosano and his death squad. Certain landowners used Rosano to intimidate people, and then they disclaimed any connection. On his motorbike Sgt. Rosano terrorized the surrounding areas; he and his gang were reputed to have killed more than fifty people. He was employed by the military, though when any specific command was confronted about him, they always pointed to some other command as being his controllers.

The small Christian communities of the parish of Oringao met and decided to back Juanito Serrantes. They arranged a day that they would all converge on his rice field, each carrying some rice seedlings. Together they would plant the rice paddy in the name of Juanito Serrantes. With them went Fr. Brian Gore, the Australian parish priest of Oringao; Fr. Itik Dangan, the assistant priest in Kabankalan; and Fr. Romeo Empestan, also a curate in Kabankalan Parish. When they reached the rice field, Rosano was there with his men, dressed in fatigues and carrying high-powered automatic rifles. The group of peasants approached singing. With a certain trepidation they entered the field and began to plant. Each one felt the very tense silence. What would Rosano do?

Sgt. Rosano and his men remained rooted to the ground. They did not move. Not a shot was fired or a farm knife raised that day, and Juanito Serrantes got back his field. The strange thing was that when I talked with Fr. Gore afterward, I was surprised that he was not too conversant with the philosophy and theology of nonviolence. He told me that they did it because it worked, and then he said, "You know we in the Christian communities in the mountains are like ants—you see one ant and you stamp on it, you see a million ants and you run."

I asked Fr. Gore and his team to help us to do something similar in our parish. A certain Anhelito—little angel—had terrorized our communities in an outlying area. It was said he had killed twenty-six people and, in some cases, had cut off their ears and eaten them. Such fear existed that many communities did not sleep in their houses but in the long grass nearby in case he and his followers should come during the night.

The solution being bruited around was to call in the NPA "to take him out." I felt this would be fatal for several reasons:

1) The NPA would certainly do a neat job, but it would result in excising the problem rather than solving it.

2) The people themselves would have failed to face the problem and the result would be more dependency, more "flight."

3) The "glorious gun" would again emerge as the savior.

4) Killing Anhelito would ultimately solve nothing. It would reinforce the idea that evil is in the person, not in the structures.

Brian and his community teachers made several visits to our parish. They briefed our leaders on the Serrantes operation. We laid our plans carefully for a non-violent arrest. (There was an arrest warrant out for Anhelito but the police, now under the military, would not implement it.)

On a given early morning hundreds of adult community members left their homes and made their way to Anhelito's house. I had sent word that I was coming to say Mass. Anhelito expected me, but not one thousand others. At the Mass I "excommunicated" him for the murders. Anhelito, realizing he was facing what was in effect a citizen's arrest, publicly admitted his crimes. He and his followers handed over a sackful of weapons and peace returned to these communities.

It gradually became clear to me that if the majority of the people had some means of expressing their desire for justice and peace then nothing could stop them. After all it was only a tiny percentage who were holding the whole population to ransom. So, when the Edsa street revolution came, in a way it did not surprise me. I always believed it was possible and dreamed of such an event. However, following Gene Sharp's methodology, it is necessary to look and to see why it was effective, insofar as it was, and why it failed, insofar as it did. Only in that way can we perfect active nonviolence as a tool for social change.

The Question of Edsa

The Edsa Event — as the February 1986 revolt against Marcos is often called because it was centered on the road called Edsa — was an amazing combination of reactive and preemptive nonviolence.

Some see Edsa as a model revolution. This it certainly was not. It opened up a democratic space within which the sort of social reforms a revolution should undertake could take place, if the political will were there. The political will so far has not been there, so Edsa is looked on with cynicism by many. Some even say it was a CIA plot to abort the real revolution. True the CIA have been meddling in Filipino politics for years but somehow Edsa was not their style and the ball bounced several times in unpredictable directions, though not so unpredictable, in my opinion, for those who have studied the dynamics of nonviolent action.

Having said that, Edsa was a momentous and historic event, as far as it went, because in fact it did what to most people a few short months before had seemed impossible: it got rid of Marcos. Imagine, it was only a few years earlier, when Marcos's dictatorship and corruption was at its height, that Vice-President Bush came to Manila to attend his inauguration and toasted Marcos's "adherence to democratic principles and to the democratic process." Marcos followed that triumph with a marvelous tour of the United States from which he returned home with world backing. The number of massacres by his soldiers increased. In Negros alone I immediately recall three massacres.

There were the Langoni Nine. Nine young boys on their way to a basketball match were arrested, stripped of their shirts, tied together, marched through the village of Inayawan and then shot dead. Our evidence shows that the military prepared a press release *before* the massacre saying that the boys were members of a communist New Peoples Army band that had attacked by sea! The callousness of the massacre—intended to instill terror—was shown by the fact that the day before the massacre one of the military officers of the unit which committed the crime was on the beach trying to rent a couple of boats. Was this to corroborate the coming press release? If things had gone as planned, those boats would have been exhibits. But Fr. Brendan O'Connell of that parish photographed the boys almost immediately after their death and rushed a press release and so preempted the military, whose own press release was withdrawn without explanation.

Then there was the Aningal massacre in Oringao parish—a family of five. And then the Escalante massacre—nineteen young people in Escalante. That was just in Negros. The rest of the eighty-seven provinces had their own massacres, and of course, the military had gunned down Benigno Aquino on the tarmac at Manila airport. This was in front of the whole world, and yet Marcos got away with it. So, for the ordinary Filipino, the idea of soft-talking his troops into lowering the guns was laughable.

After the death of Aquino, people who had belonged to that silent majority whose passivity had kept Marcos in power began to speak out. One of the first things they did was to begin to publish alternative newspapers, which they sold illegally on the street. These papers became a focus for public opinion, and they also began to report the work of the Church for liberation, which up to this point could not make its way into the papers. The New Peoples Army also had legal fronts, and they worked together with the awakened middle class, who felt not a little guilty at their own long silence and refusal to listen to the cries of protest. Then Marcos, in one of those suave interviews of his, in answer to a challenge from David Brinkley on ABC TV, agreed to call a snap election. People still did not believe he could lose because he was, as everyone knew, a past master of election fraud and the art of buying people.

Before the election a citizen poll watch group called NAM-FREL was set up with Fortich as vice-chairman. This group involved thousands of ordinary citizens; their personal tales of heroism would fill several books. Many of these people were killed in the attempt to guard the polls.[3] The original NAM-FREL had been set up thirty years before with CIA money, but this NAMFREL was an entirely different animal, a home-grown creature born in response to the oppression. Though it did get money from abroad, it was not controlled from abroad.

When it was clear that Marcos was going to steal the election, Aquino's camp considered getting arms. They could easily have done this; they had contacts and offers. But many of them had done a seminar on nonviolence given by Jean and Hildegard Goss-Mayr, and this influenced them against the arms option. In fact, Jean and Hildegard were in Manila just around the time the arms offer was made. Butz Aquino, the brother of the slain Ninoy Aquino, personally confided the arms offer to them.

A key group of the Philippine bishops had also done a seminar with Jean and Hildegard Goss-Mayr. At that seminar they got a forceful exposition of why the Church must take up the struggle of the poor and how this should be done through active nonviolence.

When Marcos announced that he had won the election, there was a storm of protest from all over the country. And the Philippine bishops did something unprecedented. They got together and produced the most radical pastoral letter they had ever written. It was radical because it was one of the first times in recent history when a whole hierarchy condemned a dictator *before* he fell. Even more radical was their unequivocal statement that to cooperate with this now illegitimate government was actually sinful. Then, and this was certainly new and radical for an official Church document, they proposed active nonviolence as *the* method to deal with the injustice. They went so far as to list examples of active nonviolence—taken from some actions the people themselves had already been doing in the previous month. No Catholic hierarchy had ever made such a statement.

Last moment attempts were made to block the pastoral letter, with Imelda Marcos going to the papal nuncio, the nuncio phoning friends in Rome, his Rome friends phoning back to certain Philippine bishops, who now stood up on the floor of the assembly and, quoting this Vatican source, tried to delay the letter till after Marcos's inauguration. The bishops refused and pushed ahead with the letter; it was read in all the churches. It had the effect that "fixer" has in the photo printing process; without it the whole people power movement would hardly have held together. Now it had not only a blessing from the Church, but clear and explicit directions as to how to overthrow Marcos.

So, when Cory Aquino called an enormous rally in historic Rizal Park in the center of Manila to protest Marcos's stealing the election and announced her plan to defy Marcos, she outlined a plan of nonviolent activism that followed closely the bishops' pastoral. Her centerpiece was that classic nonviolent strategy patented by Parnell and Davitt in the fight for Irish land reform a hundred years earlier—the boycott. She asked for a boycott of the Marcos banks and businesses. This boycott got massive support throughout the country. Shares plummeted and businessmen who for years had played ball with Marcos got scared and began to abandon him. That boycott depended on the ordinary people, now awakened, and it worked.

It was at this point that Defense Secretary Juan Ponce Enrile for his own private reasons joined Fidel Ramos, the Armed Forces of the Philippines Deputy Commander, in a revolt against Marcos. They did this not to back Cory Aquino, not to see the will of the people implemented, but to steal power for themselves. Marcos called out the army to crush them, and they would have been crushed surely but for the Edsa Event.

Edsa is the road that fronts the army camps where Enrile and Ramos took refuge. In response to a call from the Church, the people came out and blocked the way between Marcos's army and these two military camps. How they did it is history. They did it totally without weapons. They did it principally with prayers and religious images, with songs and flowers, and gifts of sandwiches. They didn't do it out of love for Ramos and Enrile. It was the pent-up feelings of years finally bursting out — a determination to get Marcos out and do so without blood. The scenes we witnessed on our televisions were really true. It did happen. The tanks stopped; the helicopters turned back. A friend of mine, Richard Deats, the secretary of the Fellowship of Reconciliation, did painstaking research into these events. A few weeks later he interviewed the soldiers. Some were afraid their own relatives were in the crowd. Some actually saw their relatives there or thought they did. Some were ashamed. Others were smitten by a spiritual force they could not deal with.

For all its subsequent failure to live up to its promise, the events of Edsa remain an example of what might happen in our world if the feelings for peace and fellowship of the human race ever get a chance to burst out. Edsa was a touch of Camelot, a touch of the Transfiguration.

Edsa certainly demonstrated that nonviolence could be effective, but it also showed the limitations of reactive nonviolence; it didn't get to the roots of the injustice. No land reform took place; no real clean-up of the judiciary took place; corruption returned. Human rights deteriorated with the total war policy of the army. The old elite were reinstated in Negros, and the peasants remained in the same condition as before.

Why? Why so little change? Part of the answer is in understanding the distinction I made earlier between preemptive and reactive nonviolence. This distinction is important.

Buber's Objection

Active nonviolence meets its acid test in the case of Nazi Germany and the extermination of six million Jews. They, the Jews, did not resist. The Jewish theologian Martin Buber wrote to Mahatma Gandhi and challenged him on this point; it is a historic letter:

In the five years which I, myself, spent under the present (Nazi) regime, I observed many instances of genuine Satyagraha (Gandhi's term which is somewhat equivalent to Active Nonviolence) by the Jews, instances showing strength of spirit wherein there was no question of bartering their rights or of being bowed down, and where neither force nor cunning was used to escape the consequences of their behavior. Such actions apparently exerted *not the slightest influence on their opponents.* All honor indeed, to those who displayed such strength of soul! But, I cannot recognize therein a maxim for the general behavior of German Jews which might seem suited to exert an influence on the oppressed or on the world. An effective stand may be taken in the form of nonviolence against unfeeling human beings in the hope of gradually bringing them thereby to their senses: but a *diabolic universal steamroller* cannot be thus withstood. . . . Satyagraha means testimony, testimony without acknowledgment — ineffective unobserved martyrdom, a martyrdom cast to the winds . . . that is the fate of innumerable Jews in Germany. God alone accepts their testimony. But, no maxim for suitable behavior can be deduced therefrom (emphasis added).[4]

Buber sees nonviolence exclusively as *reactional* nonviolence. He sees its power in its testimony — its power to move. If that is *all* nonviolence is, then it certainly *would* be ineffective, especially in today's wars where the killers seldom see their victims. That is why it is so important to make the distinction between the two types of nonviolence, which I have called reaction and preemptive.

It is important not to be put off when people pose an impossible "last ditch" situation and then triumphantly say, "So, what can nonviolence do about this?" At a seminar in Bacolod, Negros, given by Jean and Hildegard Goss-Mayr, just such a question was posed by one of the participants. A situation was described in which there appeared to be no way out of a violent response. I was wondering how Jean would deal with the question because, knowing the questioner as I did, I felt he had an a priori commitment to armed struggle and the question seemed to be contrived. But Jean surprised me. He just nodded his head slowly and raised his arms a little, making that peculiar French shrug which gives a slight sense of acceptance and even resignation. He seemed to say: "Well, I have no magic solution to that one. I'm not going to ask people *not* to defend themselves." And then he gave Gandhi's famous example: A man's family is endangered. The man has three possibilities: To run away, which Gandhi naturally condemns as cowardice and despicable; to resist violently, which Gandhi sees as superior to running away; and lastly, to resist nonviolently, which Gandhi sees as the highest form of reaction—the one we are called to.

Hildegard, Jean's wife, joined in at this stage of the discussion and said, "You know we got to know Ralph Abernathy, Martin Luther King's close associate, quite well. He told us that in the early days, Martin Luther King himself actually did carry a gun." Then Hildegard paused, because we were all a bit shocked, and then she added simply, "But there came a time when he no longer needed to carry a gun."

Not Been Tried

A peace seminar took place in one of the leading colleges in Bacolod while I was writing this book. I was asked to speak on active nonviolence. Afterward I took questions. A leading educator in the island, himself from one of the ruling families, posed the following question. I quote him quite closely:

"I am very glad I came here. I must say I was touched by the exposition on active nonviolence, but is it not true that we have tried nonviolence here in Negros against the insurgency but the insurgency hasn't gone away? It just hasn't worked."

I explained that the nonviolent action is not directed at the insurgency; it is directed at the causes of the insurgency. Otherwise you want to get rid of the symptoms but not the disease.

What I did not add, because I deemed it inappropriate, was that nonviolence has not been tried seriously in Negros at all. Otherwise those who claim to care would confront the four leading causes of the insurgency: land, democratic participation, the courts and human rights.

Land: There has been no significant land reform since Marcos left, in spite of all the talk about it. Peasants are still being put off land that was supposed to be sequestered because the owners were right-hand men of Marcos.[5] On World Human Rights Day I saw a street play done by some peasant workers in downtown Bacolod. In the play a landowner is getting the military or some private goons to throw some peasants off the land. They plead with him, but he doesn't listen and just has them all ejected using force. This was all done in a humorous style—a sort of slapstick clowning. Then the landowner steps forward to the front of the stage, looks the crowd in the eye and says, "This is what I call genuine land reform." The crowd roared.

Democratic Participation: Voting in the first local elections that took place after Cory Aquino came to power, though free from guns, was riddled with vote buying. This at a time when the governor was calling on the rebels to come down from the mountains and try the democratic way! A careful report on the La Carlota elections done by the well-known social historian Alfred McCoy and written up by him under the title "The Restoration of Planter Power in La Carlota City,"[6] gives chapter and verse of the vote buying procedure in that district. Participation in the free choosing of their representatives remains close to zero for plantation-based peasants.[7] No participation in political life means no empowerment.

The Courts: The courts remain as corrupt as ever. I know, because I have been following up cases at the prison. The notorious official who ran our own rigged court case is still in office but in a higher position!

Human Rights: The 1992 Amnesty International Report on the Philippines is entitled "The Killing Goes On."

Where can we look for hope?

[8]

Negros

The Beginnings of a Solution

The Basic Christian Communities

One day two Cebuano-speaking men arrived at my *convento* in the mountain parish of Tabugon. They came from a far distant and obscure hamlet where I had never been. They produced a sheaf of papers. The top one depicted two human figures with arrows pointing to different spots on their bodies. On top of the page was written: Justice Committee of Christian Community of Mabolo. It was a carefully made report about a child-torture incident that had taken place in a house outside their hamlet.

To understand the significance of this event we should go back a few years. Before we introduced the Basic Christian Communities, our system was to visit the larger villages for Mass several times a year on fixed dates. People from surrounding areas came to attend the Mass and have their children baptized. If for some reason the priest did not arrive, the people went home. No priest, no activity. Inapoy was one of those villages.

We set up a Christian Community in Inapoy. Now the people ran their own Sunday worship every week, blessed the dead, and visited the sick and brought them communion. In addition they set up a health committee, a catechetical committee and a justice committee. So much life came to Inapoy that remote hamlets

123

further away from Inapoy began to ask them to start a Christian Community in their areas. The result was that Inapoy now had twelve other Christian Communities as satellites to itself; Mabolo was one of those Christian Communities and had its own small justice committee. Those two Cebuano-speaking men were from that community.

They spread out the evidence before me and told me how it had been reported at their Sunday Worship Service (probably during the gospel discussion) that a certain woman had been maltreating two little children, one aged six and the other one aged four. The arrows on the paper showed where the children were burned with cigarettes and battered and where their nails were black because their little fingertips had been hit with a hammer. The other papers were documentation showing that this was no rumor but something they had carefully investigated. These simple farming folk, whom I would never have met on the personal level under the old system, now had a vision of following Christ which involved protecting those little children and all others on the margin of life. This new vision and this new organization was the result of the Basic Christian Community.

The word *basic* here is from the Latin American *de base* and refers to natural communities taken where we find them — a little hamlet, for example, or a contiguous group of homes in a squatter area, or even a group of houses in a subdivision of a city. It is a geographical unit. The word is used in contrast to a club or group where people come together from *different* areas. The challenge of the Basic Christian Communities is precisely to interact with my physical neighbor rather than search out a kindred spirit from far away. The community should not be too large or it will lose its human touch; thirty families is about right. Some prefer to call these communities Basic Ecclesial Communities to emphasize their connection with the Church, but that connection was never in doubt in the Philippines.

My introduction to them came about this way: many years ago while I was assistant priest in the enormous parish of Kabankalan, I and the other priests thought of giving the far-flung villages worship on a Sunday. I reckoned a priestless service was better than no Mass. I had these services dotted throughout the parish every Sunday, and we called them *panimbahon* (worship in the villages).

My next assignment was to give retreats to the workers in Negros. We called this retreat the Sa-Maria. I used the Sa-Maria as the training ground for *panimbahon* leaders, and we brought out a monthly supporting booklet, which helped to spread it throughout the neighboring islands of Panay, Romblon, and those parts of Mindanao where Ilonggo is spoken. I was happy with these developments. Surely more worship was good and would translate eventually into more social awareness.

But soon there were complaints from some of my fellow priests that all this spiritual activity was very well but it seemed to be having no effect on the ever-worsening social situation. When were the people going to see a connection between the spiritual and the social world?

After a six-year stint giving the Sa-Maria retreats, I was appointed to a mountain parish in southern Negros. What to do? The old approach was obviously incomplete. I decided to ask the aid of the young Filipino priests, and I invited a group of them up to my new parish to help me. They were led by Fr. Pete Hipponia. Pete spoke about the Basic Christian Communities, but before he did he addressed me: "Niall, I know you started many *panimbahons* throughout the mountains but they are not Christian Communities as such; they are what they say — worship services. But a group of worshiping Christians has to have several other characteristics before it can be called a Community." He proceeded to draw a five-pointed star on the board and indicated how each point on the star represented a different characteristic of community:

Sharing: The members share their physical goods when in need. (They also share their time and talent.)

Participation: They make decisions together.

Justice: They work together to eradicate injustice using the principles of active nonviolence.

Reconciliation: They work toward reconciliation.

Worship: They pray together.

All this is done in the context of the wider community. Since the mid 70's hundreds of these small Christian Communities have spread throughout the island of Negros. They are the point where, at long last, religion and life join hands.

If you look at their characteristics you will see a marvelous basis for a nonviolent approach to building peace in Negros.

Characteristics of the BCC's

Sharing Time, Treasure, Talent: Attention is given to the immediate needs of the community—hunger, sickness, loneliness. You might call it crisis intervention. We reached the stage in our parish in the mountain of Tabugon when I could at the end of the day put my head on my pillow knowing that because of that web of communities there was little chance of people even in a far-flung hamlet going hungry that night. And the communities also looked beyond themselves. During the great strike of sugar workers at La Carlota Sugar Mill in 1982, the Christian Communities from all over the island sent food to the hungry workers.

Decisions Are Made Together: This means participation, and the empowerment resulting from it. I remember complaining to Fr. Brian Gore in the neighboring parish of Oringao that a certain Christian Community of mine had chosen the wrong leader—an obvious oppressor. "Don't interfere," he said. "They won't reelect that person. Let them suffer—they chose her because she had a jeep they might borrow when they are sick. When they see how she blocks any attempt at social transformation, they'll choose someone else next year. Your job is just to make sure that the election is held fairly." And that is what happened. Participation brings empowerment; empowerment brings a sense of responsibility and opens up the realization that we, little as we are, can and should do something about our situation. But we should begin small. That's what a small Christian Community does. Little victories give hope.

They Work Together To Eradicate Injustice: From the beginning, the Christian Communities in Negros singled out injustice as the besetting sin. In our parish each community developed a justice committee. These committees joined together with other community justice committees when the problem was bigger than an individual area could manage. I mentioned earlier an occasion when a thousand members — large in a mountain district — from different communities came together and offered Mass before the house of a man who was terrorizing the surrounding area.

Also the communities, by keeping the idea of injustice high on their agenda, preempted many unjust situations. For example, some middlemen arrived in the parish planning to spread out among the small farmers and offer them cash if they would promise to convert their land to a non-food crop, hemp. They would supply the fertilizer and would buy the hemp at the end of the year. The growers were interviewed by the community leaders, who asked the right questions, discussed the proposition among themselves and decided not to accept. In the event, it was the right decision. Without the community leaders the growers would have gone to separate individuals and, playing on their need for immediate cash, would have won them over one by one.

In places where oppression is fierce the question of using armed struggle as a means to solve injustices will certainly arise. The community has to be very clear from the beginning that it has specifically chosen active nonviolence as its means. Its relationship with those who have chosen armed struggle as a means to overcome the injustices will be thorny and will need constant prayerful discernment. There are no easy answers here.

Reconciliation: A community cannot exist on cold justice. There is need for the warmth of forgiveness and reconciliation. This is especially necessary in any culture which puts a value on revenge. It is also valuable as the entry point for all those discussions and reflections which lead us to understand that those who oppress us are our sisters and brothers and are themselves in chains. Our ultimate aim is not to eliminate them but to change them, to set them free. The right way is to begin in a small way, within the manageable area of a Basic Christian Community. Eventually, these attitudes must be behind the social revolution which we long for and work for in Negros.

Prayer Together: This is usually put first, but we found that people sometimes stop there and don't move on to the other characteristics, like children who want the jam but not the bread. So, though we never omitted to present prayer together as essential, we presented it as the final crowning qualification rather than the first. Prayer is what gives us the grace and strength and encouragement to continue on patiently when the road is long. It is only misleading when it is the sole means used. The Spanish proverb has it right: *A Dios rogando y con el mazzo dando*, "We keep asking God but we keep working away ourselves."

Antidote to the Culture of Dependence

Christian Communities with these characteristics nourish the independence, self-reliance and self-confidence of the people. These qualities are precisely the qualities that the sugar plantation culture of Negros destroyed. Indeed, like the AIDS virus, which destroys the self-defense antibodies of the body, the sugar culture devastates the mental antibodies which help people to stand up and believe in themselves. Hence the Basic Christian Communities have the missing antidote to this pervasive disease.

The communities spread in Negros. In my parish I had some sixty; other parishes like Oringao, Hinoba-an, Kabankalan and Candoni had similar numbers. Twelve parishes gathered together and formed an umbrella group to foster the communities. We shared stories together of the marvelous rebirth of spirit among the people within the womb of these little communities.

However, not everyone was happy with these developments. In June 1979 an article appeared in the quarterly *National Security Review* by Galileo Kintanar, a military adviser on subversion. He said: "What is now emerging as the most dangerous form of threat from the religious radicals is their creation of the so-called Basic Christian Communities in both rural and urban areas. They are practically building an infrastructure of political power in the entire country."[1]

If we go back to Gene Sharp's distinction between power from above and power from below, then Colonel Kintanar was right. The communities make people aware that they can say no to oppression and violence from above. But what Kintanar did not observe was that the communities can also say no to counter-violence from below; hence the communities are the ideal womb in which nonviolent struggle for justice, for life, for peace can grow.

When we were imprisoned by Marcos, the communities of the parishes of Oringao and Tabugon met without us, their priests, and decided to walk all the way from the mountains to Bacolod Provincial Jail to protest the imprisonment. They were joined eventually by all the small Christian Communities on the island in this nonviolent protest march. Five thousand people walked over sixty miles in the steaming tropical heat. Many more thousands lined the roads to give them water and food. It was a massive and beautiful demonstration of awakened spirit, quite unthinkable a few short years before. They called the march *Exodo.*

The Christian Communities have given the peasants a voice and that is why the military have tried to eliminate them, making it almost a criminal act in some places to belong to them. In my own parish one zealous military man threatened to burn our chapels. For that reason we began to build them back from the road, where passing army trucks wouldn't notice them. I know too that in areas controlled by the New Peoples Army, some leaders are not at ease with independent Christian Communities, which they are not able to control.

In many places the military have actually succeeded in destroying communities by driving the people out of their homes and off their land through aerial bombardment.[2] Then they gather the people together in hamlets where they give them seminars and force them to join a local militia. Those who refuse to join are deemed to be cadres of the New Peoples Army. This forced evacuation happened in the municipality of Himamaylan and resulted in the deaths of several hundred children. It happened in many others towns too, Candoni, Sipalay, Sta. Catalina, for example. But the idea and the vision are here to stay; in the long run the idea and the vision are stronger than guns and bombs. The fierce opposition to the Christian Communities is surely a sign that they are going in the right direction, leading us into the way of peace.

In 1991, in Tagaytay, outside Manila, the whole Philippine hierarchy met for a month-long plenary council with leading laity and priests and declared the Christian Community Movement "a great hope" for the Philippine Church.[3] This historic position came within months after General Raymundo Jarque's Operation Thunderbolt, which forced thirty thousand people to leave their homes and wiped out many of the Christian Communities.

Though Christian Communities are the right background and seedbed for a strategy of active nonviolence, they are not in themselves active nonviolence. They must be coupled with specific long-term strategies, such as the push for land reform, for political participation, for a clean judiciary. They must be accompanied by short- and medium-term tactics such as boycotts, fasts, non-cooperation, nonviolent intervention. And they must have the spiritual resources to meet the inevitable increase in repression which comes their way.

They also must know how to get the media and the other groups on their side, both national and international. In fact, it has been international media attention and groups like Amnesty International which have time and again helped the struggle in Negros. The soldiers have no scruples about burning down a remote mountain village, but their officers in Manila will have a lot to say if this gets out to the press. Here are two examples:

The army had burned down the hamlet of Locotan, a faraway village in Magballo Parish. We asked for a meeting with Colonel Lozada, the army chief in Bacolod. Bishop Fortich attended. He always listened carefully to what the military had to say. The army chief asked his subordinate from Magballo if it were true that the houses had been burned. "Not at all sir. I have just come this moment directly from there. No house is burned." We were flabbergasted. We knew he was lying through his teeth, but what could we do?

Then the door opened and Fr. Brendan O'Connell arrived with a brown envelope under his arm. "I've just come from Magballo," he said. "Yesterday I took these photos and developed them in my own house." He threw some photos on the table: the burned hamlet of Locotan. Colonel Lozada was livid and began to shout at his subordinate. It was an award-winning performance, but we didn't mind. We had made our point before the bishop, who in those early days naturally would believe a well-spoken military man unless there were concrete evidence to the contrary.

In more recent years, when some of us received death threats, the Philippine Human Rights Commission did not bother to investigate till Amnesty International protested in Washington and Ambassador Pelaez became embarrassed at the media questions. He called the Human Rights Commission in Manila, which then came to Negros.

For their survival, the little communities must let the larger community know what is going on.

Antidote to the Culture of Silence

At the heart of the main methods of the Christian Communities is gospel reflection. This means taking the gospel of the day or week and reading it prayerfully *as a community* and then discussing how the values it portrays, or the problems it poses, are absent from or present in their own little community.

When I first produced the *panimbahon* booklet, before we started the Christian Communities, I used to print a fixed sermon. It tended to be a doctrinal exposition or exegesis of that particular gospel passage. Fr. Frankie Connon, a Redemptorist, begged me not to print the sermon but to allow the people to have a shared homily through which they could draw the lesson from the gospel. I recall that I refused point-blank and suggested that Frankie produce the booklet himself. I just couldn't conceive that the people would be able to do this without having studied.

How wrong I was. They have studied in the school of life, and they are wonderful at applying the gospel to the daily problems. We had a gospel discussion on the passage where Jesus tells the people in Nazareth that his mission is to bring good news to the poor and liberate the oppressed, a good reading for focusing on injustice in the community. At the end of the passage, the people of Nazareth bring Jesus to a cliff, intending to push him over. "But he walked through their midst." It was interesting that one of our little group picked up on that last line, not on the fact that they tried to murder Jesus but on how he avoided being murdered. He did not run away. He turned at the edge of the cliff, looked them in the face, and our contributor added, "Surely he did this with love and not with hate, and as he walked through the midst of them, he could not have done this except with love."

Bobby, the man who made this contribution had worked in Task Force Detainees looking for disappeared persons. One day while drinking coffee in a restaurant in Guanzon Street, Kabankalan, he was confronted by some men who shot him down in cold blood. For weeks he hung between life and death before he recovered. He had an ongoing struggle to put aside the cultural need for revenge. Eventually he went a step further and forgave. He experienced freshness and joy in his "new" life. I was surprised when Bobby spoke, but then I remembered what had happened to him and realized that alone of our group he could guess at Jesus' feelings as he stood surrounded at the edge of the cliff.

Another example: At one of those gospel reflections with a group of Christian Community leaders, we read the gospel of the multiplication of the loaves and fishes. This sort of gospel leads naturally to doctrinal discussions on miracles and the Eucharist. One of the women suggested that what might have happened was that many of those people in the crowd had stashed away a little food and when they saw the apostles struggling to do the impossible—share their tiny number of loaves and fishes with the crowd—they got embarrassed and ashamed; they took out what they had hidden away and began to share it with those beside them. Bread had not been multiplied but love had—a greater miracle. Surely this was a bit of personal experience from the poor; it led to a most to-the-point discussion.

A major cause of the powerful silence of so many of the educated class in Negros—who are one of the major keys to social change—is their refusal to connect the gospel with social and political life; they flee to the mountain of metaphysics. This method of the Basic Christian Communities of applying the gospel values directly to our community situation and not exclusively to our personal mores gives a heightened level of social and political consciousness, which is necessary if one is ever to realize that there is a problem. Without such awareness, discussion of what methods to use to solve it is a waste of time.

Gradually, through the communities, oppressed people gain hope and begin to see that active nonviolence is the right approach. Believing that change through active nonviolence is possible is the initial step. The next step is making active nonviolence fully effective, and this must be learned by trial and error and humble consultation with others all over the world who have traveled this road before us.

But even if we knew all the methods, the tactics and dynamics of active nonviolence, that would not be enough. The daily working out of the nonviolent approach demands a spirituality all its own.

PART III

GRASP THE
BARBED WIRE

*A Spirituality for Active
Nonviolence*

[9]

Reconciliation

Do Not Speak to Us of Reconciliation

I agreed to give a talk on active nonviolence to a Pax Christi group in Manila. In my bones I knew that to attempt such a feat in one hour would only lead to gross misunderstanding. Some would be too easily convinced; others would be repelled. I knew the journey into active nonviolence should be a long process. No learning can take place unless it is related in some way to the experience of the hearer, and that takes time. Nevertheless, I agreed.

At the blackboard I attempted to give what I called a geography of active nonviolence, to draw a map on the board and show the different elements of active nonviolence which should appear on that map. Having placed "passion for justice," "philosophy of nonviolence," "scriptural basis for nonviolence," and so on, I then wrote "reconciliation." I had hardly written it when a Sister rose up and asked me with blazing eyes:

"How can you speak of reconciliation to the victims of Langoni? How can you speak of reconciliation to the victims of Escalante? They have never even had their cases heard. The government and army have shown no sign of sorrow or given any compensation—and you propose reconciliation?"

I was embarrassed and angry—embarrassed that she had chided me publicly as if I were unspeakably hardhearted and had no understanding of what the victims had suffered. But I was also angry with her—an intelligent woman deeply involved for long years in the struggle for justice—that she was so quick to assume that what I meant by the word *reconciliation* was a shallow reconciliation of the type that was being pushed by opportunist politicians all over the Philippines. I was also angry at myself for agreeing to the talk.

But she was only voicing the feelings of a great number of people who have witnessed so much political "reconciliation," from the hasty reconciliation of collaborators after World War II to the almost instant reconciliation of many of Marcos's right-hand men with the Filipino people after Cory Aquino took over. Their frustration and anger is expressed in this poem by J. Cabazares[1]:

> Talk to us about reconciliation
> Only if you first experience
>   the anger of our dying.
>
> Talk to us of reconciliation
> If your living is not the cause
>   of our dying.
>
> Talk to us about reconciliation
> Only if your words are not products of your devious
>   scheme
>   to silence our struggle for freedom.
>
> Talk to us about reconciliation
> Only if your intention is not to entrench yourself
>   more on your throne.
>
> Talk to us about reconciliation
> Only if you cease to appropriate all the symbols
>   and meanings of our struggle.

These are angry words, obviously coming from bitter experience.

I told the Sister that I accepted the fact that the word *reconciliation* had been prostituted. But I felt that the fact that the *word* had been hijacked and manipulated to suit the needs of some people should not stop us from reclaiming it and using the concept in its true and original meaning and force.

In its genuine sense, reconciliation must be somewhere among the cards Christian peace-builders hold in their hands. Obviously it should not be the first card to be played, and in fact normally it will be the last to be played. But it must be played or *intended* to be played sooner or later, or we have given up the struggle to initiate the Kingdom of God. But first, some examples of this false reconciliation, because it is so prevalent.

It was common in the mountain parish of Tabugon, Kabankalan, Negros Occidental, where I was parish priest, for some small landowners of twelve acres or so to find that their land was taken from them or at least encroached upon by big neighbors or lowlanders who had influence with the government officials who issue land titles. Sooner or later a personal letter would arrive to the "small" person, the victim, from a barrio captain or even a judge and the person would be requested to come before that august person and meet his antagonist; this official would help solve the problem and reconcile the two.

The problem was always presented not as a case of injustice but rather as a case of broken human relations or a breakdown in communications. The job to be done was to *mend the relationship*, not to undo the injustice. Invariably the "little" man was clapped on the back, cajoled, reassured and led to shake hands with his oppressor, although no reversal of the injustice had taken place.

This, in the Ilonggo language, is called "*patapan-tapan*" — a smoothing over. For generations the cowed people have been browbeaten and duped into this "*patapan-tapan*"; sometimes a priest or bishop would be asked to be present to give an added air of legitimacy to such spurious settlements. It was a sign of the changing times that in the case of the Bago incident (in which the peasants had sown vegetables on unused sugar land), when these peasants were summoned to meet the landowners, the latter realized that with Fr. Saguinsin and Bishop Fortich present, the *patapan-tapan* ruse was not possible and so they arrested the people at gunpoint. The *patapan-tapan* was the kid glove concealing the mailed fist.

An incident which took place when I first moved to Tabugon will illustrate just how the feudal attitude mentally bound the poor and made them ready victims for this false reconciliation.

Maximo was a poor Cebuano living in the rocky part of Tabugon. His house was burned down by a neighbor, and after a good deal of discussion in which the *convento* was involved, the man who burned the house agreed to pay one hundred fifty pesos (about fifteen dollars at that time). The man who burned the house was of more consequence than Maximo, and he would normally have gotten away with no such inquiry. He must have gone to the barrio captain when our adjudication did not suit him, because Maximo got a letter summoning him to the captain's house. Maximo complied immediately, as if it were a court order.

There at the captain's house, surrounded by all the barrio officials, he was browbeaten. Eventually he signed a document in English saying he was accepting fifty pesos willingly. Then they gave him only thirty pesos. Finally they did a bit of back-slapping and, congratulating each other that the parties had been reconciled; they all had some Tanduay rum — for which Maximo paid with the thirty pesos.

When Maximo came and told me the story, I was tempted to explode because he had signed a document in English — a great way of bamboozling the people — but I could see the shame in his eyes, so I said nothing.

However, a group of parish leaders sat down and point by point went through what had happened to see what we could learn from it. It became clear to us that a great amount of subsequent violence could be avoided at this early stage if people were able to speak up for themselves and answer back instead of accepting the injustice and going away aggrieved and then possibly months or years later evening the score by a furtive knifing. Revenge for perceived injustice is one of the commonest causes of murder in the Philippines.

Confusing Reconciliation and Forgiveness

Another problem with reconciliation is the danger of confusing it with forgiveness. Forgiveness is at the heart of Christ's message. It is a nonnegotiable condition for being a Christian. The theme occurs again and again in the gospels: "Forgive us our sins as we forgive those who sin against us," "Nor will your heavenly Father forgive you unless you forgive your enemies from your heart." And, of course, there is Jesus' own example on the cross when, though his tormentors showed no sign of sorrow, he said unilaterally: "Father, forgive them for they know not what they do."

Obviously, Christians are bound to forgive, but this Christian imperative is frequently manipulated by some in order to escape the consequences of their actions.

We organized a *daigon* — a carol-singing choir. At the Christmas season the choir would go from house to house singing the traditional carols and getting a little bit to eat and a few coins for some good cause. When the *daigon* arrived outside the house of a certain sugar planter, one of the sons emerged; he held a gun in his hand, and with an oath he shot into the crowd wounding and maiming forever the arm of my friend Erning. We helped Erning with the court case, but we could get nowhere; the judge boarded with the in-laws of the shooter. And the young *hacendero* now claimed that Erning had attacked him and produced a knife with Erning's name scratched on it! He himself filed a case against Erning.

A year or so later, the same young *hacendero* held up my Volkswagen at the point of a gun and struck my friend Junior, who was driving at the time. He then absconded with the automobile. We got the police and went to the house of the perpetrator; there was my white Volkswagen outside the front door, but the police were afraid to go in the gate, afraid, they said, of the dogs. We ignored the dogs and went in ourselves and took the car and went home to the Columban headquarters at Batang, Himamaylan. The priests happened to be gathered for the annual retreat, so we discussed together what to do. We decided that since Erning, the man who had been disabled, had never been able to work again (he had been a secretary-typist), and since his court case was getting nowhere, we would take an unusual step: We ourselves would file a case in court against the *hacendero* because we had him cold on the crime of carnapping—a serious matter in law.

It took several years before the case was called, and I was actually subpoenaed to witness. As I sat on the witness stand, the defendant's lawyer led me through a series of questions culminating with the following exchange:

Lawyer: Fr. O'Brien, do you believe in the teaching of the Roman Catholic Church?
Me: Yes.
Lawyer: Fr. O'Brien, do you teach the teachings of the Roman Catholic Church?
Me: Yes.
Lawyer: Fr. O'Brien, would you tell the court if you teach the church's teaching on forgiveness?
Me: Yes.
Lawyer: Fr. O'Brien, are you not willing to forgive this man?

I was allowed to answer only yes or no. So I turned to the judge and asked whether I could explain. He allowed my request.

"From the start," I said, "I have forgiven Juan for what he did. There is no withholding of forgiveness here; I have forgiven him and he is in my prayers. But we priests met and decided to take this case for the safety of ordinary people, because Juan is alleged to have done many acts like this and if no one takes a case he will go on doing them." Then I added, not too ingenuously, "Some priests said there is no justice in the courts, but I said that I am sure there is, and this would surely prove it." And I smiled with confidence at the judge.

Our case went on for ten years; finally it just disappeared and the court stopped calling us. The case was never concluded. The court records do not exist. A few years later the judge in the first case (the shooting case) called Erning and Juan and said in court, "Today is my birthday; I have decided to give you both a gift: *patas kamo* — 'You are both quits' — case closed." My friend Erning never worked again.

Reconciliation Is the Kingdom in Practice

One night during our stay as guests of the State in Bacolod Provincial Jail — a story I have told elsewhere[2] — there was a riot.

The guards were drunk and tried to take out two prisoners from the cells: Moldez Diaz and Nene Martinez, who was head of cell nine.

Moldez handed himself over, but Nene would not budge. The other prisoners refused to open the gate. The guards got rough and fired their guns; the prisoners in all the cells responded immediately by smashing the light bulbs and barricading the cell gates and even managing to electrify the gates by connecting the electric light wires to them. The guards called in the military. Soon the prison yard was swarming with some two hundred soldiers in battle gear: shields, M16 assault rifles, tear gas and ominous white bands on their foreheads, to distinguish themselves when the firing started.

Colonel Geolingo demanded that the barricade be taken down. Nene Martinez, faced with all these troops said simply, "We won't take down the barricade till you hand back Moldez." Colonel Geolingo, without a word, handed back Moldez, the barricades were taken down, and the troops withdrew. . . .

Next morning I saw Nene Martinez sitting on his hunkers outside the cell, his head on his hands, looking out into the middle distance.

"What are you thinking of?"

"I am thinking of the guards," he said.

In the way he said it, I could feel hate and anger. I said: "Nene, I was moved by the way you stood up for Moldez last night. You took a risk for a friend that I don't know that I would have taken. I also feel angry with the guards; after all, many of us could have been killed last night. But the way I feel is that when all is said and done, the guards are really victims like ourselves and ultimately they are our brothers. If ever I were to allow myself to forget that, my twenty years in the Philippines would be undone."

Looking back, my words were ahead of my deeds, because I myself got mad with the guards publicly several times. In the midst of the fray I did not remember that being brothers and sisters is at the heart of evangelization and that the task before us is precisely the rediscovery, the restoration and the regaining of this fellowship, this being one family in God. Every time we do this or avert the opposite, we are initiating the Kingdom of God, the Peaceable Kingdom where the lion lies down with the lamb. Suddenly, passages in the scriptures that we never noticed before leap out at us, as in Ephesians:

> For Christ is our peace, he who had made the two peoples one, destroying in his own flesh the wall—the hatred— which separated us. He abolished the Law with its commands and precepts. He made *peace* in uniting the two peoples in him, creating out of the two one New Man. He destroyed hatred and *reconciled* us both to God through the cross, making the two one body.
>
> He came to proclaim *peace*; peace to you who were far off, peace to the Jews who were near. Through him we— the two peoples—approach the Father in one Spirit (Eph. 2:14-18) (emphasis added).

And as in Colossians:

> Through him God willed to *reconcile* all things with himself, and through him, through his blood shed on the cross, God establishes *peace*, on earth as in Heaven (Col. 1:15-20) (emphasis added).

Suddenly, we realize that reconciliation seems to be the ulti· mate aim of the coming of Jesus—restoring the world to the dream God had for it from the beginning. We see that the work of reconciliation, the work of "propagating the gospel of peace" is the work to which all Christians are called, that being a Christian means being a reconciler and engaging in the peacebuilding which leads to the Kingdom.

> The Kingdom of God is not a matter of eating and drinking, but of justice, peace and the joy that is given by the Holy Spirit. . . . Let us, then, make it our aim to work for peace and to strengthen one another (Rom. 14:17-19).

[10]

Forgiveness

First Step to the First Steps

Who Will Stop the Spiral of Hate?

In 1981 soldiers of the Long Range Patrol attached to the Canlaon Task Force, caught an eighteen year old boy, Romeo, in Barrio Canlamay. Romeo was carrying a secret message for the NPA telling of the Canlaon Task Force's movements. Romeo was the son of a man who had given evidence against the Long Range Patrol in a case where they were accused of torturing seven peasants by forcing them to eat star apples till their stomachs almost burst and then shooting them and burying them before they were completely dead. To embitter the case, it was said that, though there was no doubt about the central events, the evidence given by this particular witness was partly false.

The soldiers tortured Romeo and paraded him before the people at Sitio Gusnit. When the Gusnit people last saw him he was walking in line with bloody feet and tears were streaming down his face. Days later they found his body at the Hilabangon River. The skin had been hacked from his feet, his hands were cut off. His head was missing. They brought his body back and buried it at Gusnit. Romeo became a hero in rebel circles and songs were sung about him telling how, in spite of the torture, he had not divulged the whereabouts of the rebels. And when the local mayor and his bodyguards were killed by the NPA, a short time later, one of the assailants was heard to cry out, "this is for Romeo."

The motives for all the killings and torturings at one level can be presented in ideological terms. At another level they can be presented as part of a relentless spiral of revenge. Both levels interact.

The word for revenge in Ilonggo is *timalos* or *balos*—it is a powerful cultural trait and after twenty years of killing, the number of people who have revenge as a motivation—independent of any ideological or idealistic consideration—has grown large. Sweet reason, which had some say in the early stages, has diminished and *timalos*, the blind and furious and patient passion for revenge, complicates every situation.

One wonders how peace can ever return when so many families have lost members—sometimes by the most cruel means of having their heads cut off or livers cut out. Even if a semblance of equity were introduced into Negros, could people on both sides forget what and who they had lost in these terrible years?

Even granted that conditions for reconciliation were objectively realizable, the residue of hate and personal hurt is so great that some people cannot even look at one another without revulsion; beginning a dialogue is out of the question. There is an impasse. Only one thing can break that impasse: forgiveness.

While in prison, we asked the Carmelite Sisters who made our vestments to make a special Mass stole for each of us. The design showed a dove hovering over barbed wire, looking for a place to land. A hand has grasped the barbed wire, making a spot for the dove to land. So it is, we felt, that in the growing spiral of anger and hate and war, some people must grasp the sharp barbs and absorb the pain and give space for the dove of peace to descend upon the earth.

I do not want to give the impression that the only choice is between revenge and forgiveness. Not so at all. It is quite possible to have no plans or ideas of any sort of revenge but still be unwilling or unable to forgive (I speak here of forgiving on my own behalf insofar as an act has been done against me). However, in a culture where revenge is endemic — it is so in Negros — the first step must be to forswear revenge and hate. I contend that if we do this consciously, if we do what is within our power, then we may be given the grace to do what is not within our unaided power — the grace to forgive. Because forgiveness is not reasonable, it needs something more than reason to evoke it — it needs grace.

Forgiveness is at the heart of the Christian message — being forgiven and forgiving. In fact, it is the only condition given to Christians for receiving forgiveness: first they must forgive.

Attacking the Heart and the Conscience

It's easy enough to talk about forgiveness, but it cannot be pushed on others. The act of forgiveness is a wholly personal act; no one can do it for another. One cannot assemble an oppressed people and forgive the enemy on their behalf — as I have seen done by a zealous priest. What we can and should do is exhort them to forgive their enemies with the carefully underlined precaution that we are not once again asking them to draw back from the arduous process and task of seeking restitution and genuine reconciliation.

Let us look again at the case of the De los Santos family, the family from the town of Himamaylan massacred while asleep — the case that reached President Aquino. Joaquin, the eldest boy, survived. From his position on the floor among the bodies he had witnessed the soldiers stealing their belongings. Joaquin was brought, even before the burial, to stay with me in order to attend the hospital for his shattered arm. Also, since he was a witness to what happened, his uncles and aunts wanted him out of danger.

When the day for the burial came, it was agreed that Joaquin would return incognito to the town of Himamaylan for the funeral and that he would give a message during the Mass, but his message would be on tape. He would watch the funeral Mass from the sanctuary, standing behind the twenty or thirty con-celebrating priests.

The whole Mass was carefully prepared by the parish workers of Himamaylan. Beforehand I discussed with them the need for the liturgy to be, in the words of Jean Goss-Mayr, an attack on the heart and the conscience. My remarks were presumptuous; they had already conceived the same plan. The theme was that the suffering of one is the suffering of all. They had these words in Ilonggo — *Kasakit sang isa, kasakit sang tanan* — in big letters behind the altar. The sufferings of the people were presented through various symbols during the Mass, and the murders were roundly condemned, though any note of revenge or hate was excluded. At the offertory imitation machine guns were burned before the altar in a whoosh of flame. When Joaquin's talk was announced, he did not appear, just his voice was heard over the loudspeaker system. He said two things, surely addressed to the soldiers, "I have no desire for revenge." (I think he added, "I wouldn't be able to even if I wanted.") He finished with "Father forgive them for they know not what they do."

A strange thing is said to have happened in the next few days. Before I tell it, let me say that in all my years in the Philippines, I have not personally known of military men regretting or com-pensating for what they have done, not because it has not hap-pened but because I have never been close enough to them to know these things. But now three Scout Rangers, each on dif-ferent occasions, approached the commanding officer of the camp and said that the killing of Morit de los Santos's family was wrong. One was allegedly shot in the back as he left the camp. Another disappeared, and the third announced he was going to Manila to denounce his fellow Scout Rangers.

I like to think that maybe, since some soldiers in civilian clothes were at that thronged Mass, those three men were among those who attended the Mass. Maybe they were moved by the liturgy and the faith which boldly pointed out the sin of the Scout Rangers, but nevertheless was not vindictive and asked God's forgiveness for them. I like to think that maybe they got the grace of repentance. I would like to believe that their hearts and consciences were touched because, on the day we are convinced that they have no hearts, on the day we see them only as demons, on that day a bit of our own humanity slips away.

Joaquin settled down in Manila and got married and started a family. But the story does not end there. Allan Berlow, a young American journalist working for the *San Francisco Chronicle*, and his wife Susan got interested in the case and followed it to the ends of the earth, so to speak—going to far-off islands to interview the families of the three soldiers. Berlow discovered that the Philippine Army in its dispatches actually had glorified the massacre as a military encounter, and one military inquiry proposed honoring the participants in the massacre with a citation for bravery.[1]

Following up the case was not easy because in the meantime the Scout Rangers had been abolished for their participation in one of the seven coups against President Corazon Aquino. Their commander during the massacre, Captain Melvin Gutierrez, had been sent by the military to do further training in Oklahoma in the United States. Berlow finally caught up with Gutierrez after his return, in Davao City in the far south of the Island of Mindanao. He asked him about the soldier who was said to have been shot dead for protesting the massacre. Yes, Gutierrez remembered him very well. He was killed by his own hand. He had committed suicide. Why then, Berlow asked, had the dead soldier's wife received an official death certificate saying he was killed in an encounter with the NPA? Well, that was to ensure she would get her widow's pension.

When I was going through the debris of the house a couple of days after the massacre and a few days before the funeral, I picked up a cheap plaster crucifix. It had fallen from the family shrine. The body of Christ had been smashed in the hail of bullets.

[11]

Stumbling Blocks

To Give or Not To Give

"What use is all the faith in the world if it doesn't result in stretching out our hand to the hungry and oppressed around us"—a rough translation—but accurate of James 2:14. "Such faith is worthless." So many people working for justice and peace feel angry at the sight of religious people who don't care about the poor. This can lead us at times to downgrade the importance of our faith and the things that nourish it. It may be time for a retreat or prayer, and I say "little good all that prayer and devotion has done so and so." But that would be a fatal attitude. For disciples it is precisely our faith which gives the impetus to us to go out and *do*. As the old spiritual books used to say, we must struggle to be both Mary and Martha at the same time. Neglect of our own faith dimension will surely affect our activity dimension.

Workers for justice have reserved special animosity for those Christians whom they claim destroy the poor with handouts. They say they are worse than those who ignore the poor and oppressed altogether. Even Mother Teresa does not escape the censure of the more severe. But we forget that we ourselves surely began our outward journey by first being moved by the plight of others and giving a handout. Later we realized that this was not only not enough, but possibly damaging. However,

153

the handout mentality is a stage along the way, and we should try to lead people to the next level, not by condemning them but by explaining to them the need for social and political analysis.

We have to show them that without some analysis our handout of, say medicine, might be doing more harm than good. In a hospital in Negros the chief nurse was a friend of all of the Columbans. We gave her medicines to be used for indigent people. She used them, but she also took on the hospital administration and reported them to higher authorities to force them to release the medicines that the government was giving for the poor but which were not reaching them. If she did not do this, our gift of medicines would have only aided and abetted the overall stealing by the officials of medicines meant for the poor. Compassion now must go hand in hand with a hardnosed examination of who is doing what to whom.

The Nicodemus Clause

Another stumbling block for those working for justice is the frequency with which they see the rich align themselves with the oppressors. It seems as if Marx's insight that people always align themselves on a basis of class interest is an inexorable and ironclad law. A knowledge of the social history of Negros, as portrayed for example in Violeta Lopez-Gonzaga's book *The Socio-Politics of Sugar: Wealth, Power, Formation, and Change in Negros* shows us just how true this has been over the years. History and personal experience join in saying that that is how it has always been; reason seems to say this is also how it will inevitably be. Yet, there are exceptions: Nicodemus and Zacchaeus are two. Zacchaeus did an about-face when he met Jesus. He not only repented and gave up his extortion, but he promised publicly to compensate his victims fourfold. Nicodemus, like all of his class, stood to lose materially if he followed Jesus. At first he would only meet Jesus secretly and at night, but ultimately he made the break and took a public stand by claiming the criminal's body. There are enough examples throughout history to show that we are not irrevocably determined by our class interests. The fact that there can be an exception to that apparently iron-clad rule I like to call the Nicodemus clause.

A group of Negrenses, landholders all, asked me to a special meeting they were having. They were being taxed or harassed by the New Peoples Army or young armed men who claimed to be acting for the New Peoples Army. The same landowners and planters, though not classic large holders, were important enough middle holders. They were being pressured by the army and their peers to arm the peasants on their farms or to accept military units on their farms. These units would be made up either of soldiers or of their civilian-based surrogates: the Civilian Armed Forces Geographical Units called CAFGUs.

Several young Filipino priests attended the meeting with me; it was a solemn and serious meeting. There were about eight couples present, each of them a landowner, each of them, over the years, had struggled to be Christian. They had remained faithful to Bishop Fortich during that time in spite of the attacks against him and themselves for supporting him. The meeting took place in the roomy *sala* of the house of one of the group. The walls of natural stone were hung with oil or watercolor paintings done by the family or by friends. The meeting began with one of the group reading the Sermon on the Mount from St. Matthew.

Then one member explained simply the situation on his own hacienda. Members of the New Peoples Army or their surrogates were pressing him to pay taxes for their support. He was refusing. The military was pushing him to introduce militia; his brother was hardly talking to him because he would not go along with him and other *hacenderos* in organizing the militia. A neighboring landowner threatened to cut off his right of way. He had nevertheless decided that under no condition would he bring in armed militia.

Then another member spoke. He wasn't so sure. He would do his best to avoid getting into arms, but he felt he did have the right of self-defense.

Then another spoke, or his wife did first, and he obviously, by his nods, agreed with her. She said that a year ago they had armed their *encargado*—the man who runs the plantation for them—but he had ended up by shooting dead one of their own laborers. They felt responsible. "Since then we have made the decision that we would rather lose our land and even our lives rather than get into guns." She looked over to her husband who nodded quietly. Not all agreed, but by the time all had spoken it was clear that three couples had made a firm decision never to resort to arms.

Then one of them said: "We have been saying what we will not do, but what can we *positively* do? We are all paying the legal minimum wage, but that is not enough. It's not a family wage; it's not a living wage." The conversation took that positive turn.

I was surprised. It was clear by the tone of voice and the serious atmosphere of the whole group that every word was said in earnest. I also felt humbled. I had so long held to the Nicodemus clause but rarely witnessed it so clearly. When I added my points about the real meaning of turning the other cheek, I did so with diffidence, knowing I was speaking from a position less vulnerable than theirs and asking them to do what was not being asked of myself.

Some will say that these are the exceptions among the *hacenderos*, and that is true. But there are enough *hacenderos* like this to prove that gospel story of Nicodemus and Zacchaeus true in real life today and to give the lie to the rigid outlook that says the rich can never change. Enough of them in Negros changed to present Fortich with a plaque saying:

For over two decades, you have been a part of our lives. You have known us as children, as parents and as grandparents. You have always welcomed everyone; your heart and home is open to all. . . .

But, when you started to remind us of our Christian obligations to our laborers and employees; when you responded to the plight of the poor, the landless and the oppressed; when the promotion of social justice became the thrust of your pastoral programs, many started to part ways with you.

A number of us became disillusioned with you. Many felt betrayed. There were those who wanted you to attend only to our spiritual needs, to preach only of love and brotherhood, not of justice and social transformation.

But it is also true that there were those among us who began to share your vision and continued to believe in what you preached. It is also true that through your word and deeds, some of us took the initiative to alleviate the social inequity in our Negros situation. ... Your work as our Bishop has inspired us to become better Christians through an awareness of the unjust structures of our society. And you have challenged us to work for change.

Thus, we of the planters group who have chosen to trust in your wisdom and guidance — thank you.[1]

The Conflict Is Structural

If it's true that the rich are powerfully influenced but not relentlessly determined by class or any of the other hidden mechanisms of life to act in such and such a way, it is also true that the poor have no monopoly on virtue. After we have gotten over a Calvinistic prejudice that poverty is in some way related to personal guilt, we may find ourselves idealizing the poor ... and then going through a "flip" when we are let down by someone we have tried to help or when we find the poor as prone to injustice and betrayal as the rest of us. They are members of the human race. We must avoid the delusion of setting them on a pedestal because our disillusion will be in proportion to our original illusion.

I recall a case in the parish of Tabugon when we had worked very hard to get a poor old woman's land back for her. A comfortably off absentee landowner had taken advantage of her and had repossessed her water buffalo and her land. The absentee landowner also had some legal rights (the right to a water buffalo calf among them), and while we presented the case of the old woman, we guaranteed to protect these rights. We won the case and to my amazement, when it came time for the old woman to fulfill her part of the bargain — handing over the calf — she refused to do so. She felt, it seems to me, that she had the other woman on the run. I can recall her steely gaze as I told her we would not have helped her in the first place if we knew this would be the outcome. She was unmoved.

Or take another case where a widow of a New Peoples Army fighter with a large family told us how she discovered that her widow's rice ration was being stolen by the cadres who were supposed to deliver it. And yet another case where a labor union leader who gave many seminars on the rights of the workers and the evils of management was entrusted with checks belonging to the workers; he stole them and pretended he had lost them. I verified the case carefully and went to one of his co-workers and explained. He said: "Yes, it is true, but we must not forget that he has laid his life on the line for the cause!" Up till recently he was still getting a handsome salary for the cause.

All this reminds us that the problem in Negros is not between good and bad people but is a *structural* conflict between rich and poor. "Structurally," as Albert Nolan says, "the cause of the poor and oppressed is right and just no matter what individual poor people may be like."[2] We side with them, we take an option for the poor, not because they are good but because that is what the Kingdom is about; it means removing the structures which turn societies, like that in Negros, into ones that put us at each other's throats.

When we locate evil in persons themselves rather than in their actions, we prepare the way for terrible crimes. When we locate evil in structures, we open the way to the sort of change that will release the captors from their own chains, not eliminate them.

It is a cop-out to run away from the dilemma posed by the fact that good and bad people are on both sides, to say "a plague on both your houses, both left and right."[3] That seems to leave the speaker squarely in the middle. But it's not as simple as that. True, the man who joins the New Peoples Army kills as surely as the soldiers who massacred the civilians at Langoni or Escalante. Nevertheless, the moral stricture on the two acts will be different. Walter Wink makes the same point about South Africa:

> Likewise, blanket denunciations of violence by the churches place the counter-violence of the oppressed on the same level as the violence of the system that has driven the oppressed to such desperation. The Kairos Document pointedly asks: "Would it be legitimate to describe both the physical force used by a rapist and the physical force used by a woman trying to resist the rapist as violence?[4]

No church has the moral right to condemn violence unless it has condemned the injustice that gives rise to it. In South Africa, to the degree that a church has remained silent about apartheid, it has forfeited its right to condemn the African National Congress.

The Church, a Scandal?

But one of the greatest of all stumbling blocks for peacebuilders is the scandal they feel when their own church leaders do not support them or when their ecclesiastical leaders always take the side of the rich. Ever since Constantine this has been the tendency, and the Philippines has been a prime example. What to do? It is not just a mental dilemma. A young Filipino priest whose bishop publicly makes it clear that he does not support him could be put in real danger to his life as the normal protection that goes with being a priest in good standing is removed. So also, the lack of a church blessing can put the life of church activists in danger.

Church superiors have an answer: "You don't consult us when you make decisions, then you blame us when we don't come to rescue you from positions you've got yourself into without consulting us." When this protest is genuine, it is an argument for moving, at times, more slowly in order to preserve the unity of the Church in an important issue.

When we were first imprisoned, Bishop Fortich asked us to come out of prison under house arrest, leaving our lay companions inside the prison. We were in a dilemma. To leave them inside surely meant a form of betrayal—we get the easy option of living at home under house arrest, while our followers have to endure prison. We had a dramatic encounter with Bishop Fortich in the prison itself. He said, "This crime (multiple murder) is legally unbailable; if some of you accept house arrest, it will undermine the unbailability of the crime and a judge must grant bail to *all.*"

But we knew there was something else at stake as well. We were in danger of dividing the Church which at that moment had a powerfully united stand. The bishop had wangled this house arrest out of Marcos by threatening to stop all Masses. If we refused, we would make the bishop look weak before Marcos: "His own priests won't obey him." Nevertheless, we felt strongly that to come out was shameful. Others who took a more radical stand would say, "See these priests led you down the road and then abandoned you."

We solved our dilemma, but not our anguish, by leaving the decision to our companions. They decided we should go out of prison on house arrest, and they would remain.

It turned out the bishop was wrong; coming out did not persuade the judge to give bail to all. But what did happen was that during that vital interval while we waited in vain for the bail decision, the bishop and the Church realized that we were right and willingly accepted our return to jail and this time backed us all the way. It was this *united* backing that helped us to win through eventually. The wrong decision was right.

It is a terrible tragedy when bishops and priests and lay people are divided; it results in a sort of "balkanization" of the community. Under such circumstances no work for peace through justice can prosper. So everything should be done to avoid it. Being forced to wait may be painful, but when the green light eventually comes, there is pent-up energy developed from the waiting. Whereas if things have descended into bitter, public, mutual name-calling, by the time the green light comes, then very little is left to go forward with. I suppose I'm voting in favor of patience, but *revolutionary* patience. The patient shall possess the earth.

The vision of justice, though ignored, neglected and betrayed, is nevertheless so central to the teachings of the Church that eventually it must win through.

There are cases when some Church leaders have become spokespersons for the rich; this borders on the obscene. But even they cannot stop the priests and the faithful working for justice and peace. It is a pity to waste time and even mental and spiritual energy decrying them instead of getting on with the job. Matthew's little community seems to have had a similar problem: "The scribes and pharisees have succeeded Moses as teachers; therefore, do everything and observe everything they tell you. But do not follow their example" (Matt. 23:2–3).

But Matthew doesn't stop there, he has some special advice for resolving disputes within the community. He says that when a problem like this arises we should approach the person we think is erring privately: "If he listens, you have won your brother." Though you have "attacked his heart and conscience," you have saved him the embarrassment or even humiliation of a public attack; maybe you have also learned something by listening to his point of view.

"If he does not listen to you, take two or three others"; this raises the stakes but it is still, to a degree, private. He has a chance to see that this is not a gripe of one person and obviously the quality of the people who come together will mean something. The very act of organizing such a meeting will demand that matters are more thought out.

"If he still refuses to listen to them, inform the assembled church about him." Only at this stage do you go to a higher body.

Finally, as a last resort Matthew proposes something that

looks very like the modern-day boycott: "If he does not listen to the Church, regard him as a pagan or a publican."

We are not bound to follow Matthew literally. The essence of his advice is that the unity of the community is a pivotal value which we undermine at our peril. For that very unity gives the punch and power to our actions for peace. Matthew is aware that an early public denunciation causes more heat than light and, except for giving psychological release to the denouncer, rarely achieves its purpose. There are last-resort situations when unity cannot be preserved, but these are rare (I refer to a case where the price of unity is the certain and permanent betrayal of what the Church stands for).

In the mid 1970s, as the antagonism between the sugar industry and the Church became more acute, some *hacenderos* used every means to pressure Bishop Fortich to disown the new direction. Gradually a rift opened up between the bishop and us, his priests. The bishop became more and more isolated. Whenever we went to visit him to try and talk, we would be in the room but a few minutes when a bevy of planters and government officials would swarm in and destroy every chance of a heart-to-heart talk. Every time we priests met, the conversation would come round again to reconciliation with the bishop. So we planned an exclusive meeting at a special hour where no interruption would be possible.

The meeting was no magic wand. The bishop did not break with the planters—he has not done that to this day—though many of them broke with him. But somehow the meeting mended our relationship and eventually we forged a unity that allowed the diocese to take a concerted stand for justice, a stand that was an example to the whole Philippines.

[12]

Prayer

To Work or To Pray?

There is a moving scene in the film "Zorba the Greek." A young widow has been caught in adultery and, by village tradition, she should be stoned to death. As the woman cowers in terror and the men of the village move in to stone her, the sound of the *Kyrie Eleison* — "Lord, have mercy" — is heard from inside the old stone church where the rest of the villagers are worshiping; the chant seems to bless and encourage the stone throwers in their merciless work.

This is the opposite of what prayer is about. Prayer is contact with God, and when it is authentic the mercy of God touches the searchers and flows out on their fellows, radiating God's mercy and love to them. Therefore, in working for justice and peace, much prayer is needed. But precisely because the work itself is so all-engulfing we find that we begin to neglect prayer, with the result that sometimes we may give up completely the journey that we started out on.

Prayer for Christians means putting ourselves in contact with Jesus risen from the dead. That contact is obviously vital to a person whose faith and hope and love are each being put to a grueling test. The peace-builder has to contend with a situation of death and suffering; the peace-builder has to accept and live with the disunity and quarreling which inevitably erupt with fellow workers, and the peace-builder has to accept himself or herself—depression, physical sickness, moral weakness. It is not possible to survive in this work without the strength and grace which comes with that contact with Jesus alive—and a prime source of that contact is prayer.

I recall one young activist who did a great deal for founding a good labor union. He explained to me why he would not go to Mass on Sunday and why, even more so, he would not receive communion. "It is not possible," he said, "to receive communion with *hacenderos* who are oppressing the people." He would wait, presumably till the situation had changed and the community was purer. He did a great work for the union, was sincere in his work, but later stole large funds from the union and ran away with them, moved into business and got involved in embezzlement.

I do not recount this story to imply that I myself am a master at prayer. In fact, in writing this chapter, I feel more than a twinge of embarrassment; I feel reluctant. After all, those who write on prayer are traditionally masters of it. I am writing as one who, while working for peace and justice, has continually found myself neglecting my prayer life. It has been an uphill struggle, and I don't seem ever to have reached the top. But maybe there is a value in someone like me sharing my ideas on prayer because, at least, the reader won't feel I am speaking from the quiet of a monastery garden or from a heart that has never strayed. It is in spite of all my own failure that I reassert the necessity of prayer. As I search to find why I find it difficult, the reader might feel like a kindred spirit.

Many of us were trained in a monastic style of spirituality. Certainly that was the model for the post-Tridentine seminaries, and what was learned in the seminaries was echoed in parishes. By monastic, I mean that certain times in the day were set aside for prayer, certain times for work, certain times for recreation. Morning Mass and the Hours, Angelus, midday prayer, Vespers, and so on. But this approach presumes a quiet lifestyle, a lifestyle in which there are many fixed places and times in the day. It presumes a stability of life; it also presumes a stable political

situation. It presumes a controlled environment. But once we move into the work for peace and justice, our life can be in turmoil because we are frequently called to react to events and they dictate our timetable. So how do we get all the necessary prayer in?

It is not enough to say *"laborare est orare"* — "to work is to pray" — because that is only true if we do have time set aside for normal prayer. Jesus used to abandon his "work" to go away to a quiet place to pray.

> That evening just as the sun set, people brought to Jesus all the sick and those who had evil spirits. The whole town was gathered near the door. Jesus healed many who had various diseases, and drove out many demons; but he did not let them speak, for they knew who he was.
>
> Very early in the morning, before daylight, Jesus got up and went away to a lonely place where he prayed. Simon and the others went out, too, searching for him, and when they found him they said, "Everyone is looking for you" (Mark 1:32-37).

The point here is that Jesus abandoned sick people and left them unattended. He did this to get time to be alone and pray.

So what will become of us if we are too busy to give this time, if our work for justice does indeed make us too busy? For my part, in my parish, I developed some small helps of my own to suit my situation. Each one of us has to do this.

Also, perhaps we ought to have the courage to give contemplation a try. By contemplation I mean putting ourselves into the presence of God in such a way that almost no words at all are necessary — a glance, a word, a desire, a deliberate sense of that presence. I have heard that many simple folk with no intellectual training are particularly good at this and have unconsciously attained a high level of prayer through which they live constantly in the presence of God.

A Filipino Carmelite sister and a lay companion of hers gave a talk to the Bacolod Priests' Forum in which they explained about their apostolate, of introducing ordinary people, peasants, simple farming people in the mountains, poor people in villages and squatter areas, of introducing these people into the higher forms of prayer of St. John of the Cross. To their amazement and delight, many of these people have already been practicing some of these forms of prayer. The problem, the sister said, was that frequently some of these simple lay people were at a much higher level of prayer than their parish priest.

Abusus Non Tollit Usus

The late Jean Goss-Mayr, who spent his life working nonviolently for justice, insisted that prayer and fasting are essential ingredients in the preparation and the carrying through of any important nonviolent actions, such as demonstrations or confronting the powers or some important dialogue. Jean said it very dramatically in his talks. He did not speak any English, and he was all the more dramatic in French when he would say: "Some people say that the nonviolent life is very difficult—*they are wrong, they are lying; it is not very difficult.* [Then he would pause.] It is *impossible* [another pause] without Christ, without fervent prayer and fasting."

It always caused me anguish to find that we would hold tense meetings about the situation in Negros—tense, depressing, meetings filled with bad news about more killings, burnings, evacuations—and end filled with anger. But we did not often make prayer an integral part of those meetings.

There is, of course, another angle. At times there would be someone present who asked for prayer and more prayer but opposed any action for justice or always found reasons for delaying it. For me, such people bring prayer into disrepute and give solace to those, like my friend, who used their behavior as a reason for not going to Mass at all. Much prayer with little justice is the right recipe for atheism.

Of course, prayer can be abused. Some born-again and praise-the-Lord groups ride prayer to death. They claim every event in the day to be a result of prayer; they have no problem in ascribing their wealth to prayer. Some Charismatic groups have been used consistently in the Philippines as an escape from facing the social problems, and these groups are often promoted by the military.

The fact that some people abuse prayer in this way should not put us off. The old Latin saying is good: *Abusus non tollit usus*, "Because someone uses something badly does not mean that it cannot be used well." If prayer is misused, that should not force us to drop it.

Again and again while writing this book I have been aware that so much of what we do is a *reaction* to what someone else does. We know people who never stop talking about prayer but have scant interest in the suffering of all around us. We react ... get back at them by paying less attention to what they are always ranting about. But it's ourselves we injure. Prayer is essential in spite of the Pharisees. It is a further tragedy when we teach others our "reactions." At least *we* are reacting; we are aware of two views. But the people we teach have only one view — the reaction. It is an extreme. The holders of the opposite view now find justification for their opinion, perhaps that social actionists are godless, and so the circle of polarization is completed and strengthened.

Be Easy on Yourself

Our prayer will reflect the rest of our life. If we are over-worked, "uptight," always gasping for breath, then our personal relationships will suffer, including our personal relationship with God. I speak as one who has been guilty.

But peace-building, precisely because it is so urgent, lends itself to overwork and oppressive and humorless dedication. My advice for those who wish to give their lives to peace-building? For the love of God, have sense, go easy, do not repeat the same mistakes as the rest of us.

Change, by its nature, is gradual; if a little delay will bring a substantial number of others along, then that is worth it. A too rigid approach will often cause the sort of "flip" we talked of earlier. We are on a marathon race, not a sixty-yard dash. The road is strewn with those who tried to run too fast. The important thing is joy along the way as we relentlessly work for change — particularly change of the basic structures that give rise to injustice.

And we must have a sense of humor. We must laugh at our own weakness and the foibles of others, and be able to accept that a person can do a good job in one area while having difficulties in another. Sometimes our idea of perfection is Greek, pagan, pre-Christian. It is the perfection the Greek artists and philosophers strove for. But Jesus' idea of perfection is different: "Be compassionate," he says, "as your Heavenly Father is compassionate." So compassion, understanding, patience with ourselves and others is what we need on this marathon race. In such an atmosphere, prayer will not be a necessary burden — but a quiet joy.

We should not forget prayer to Mary; think for a moment of how appropriate an inspiration she is for peace-builders.

- Mary, tenderly holding the baby in such frugal surroundings.
- Mary, the prophet, proclaiming the Lord of Justice who puts down the mighty from their thrones and raises up the poor.
- Mary, standing at the foot of the cross, confronting the soldiers by her presence and attacking their hearts and their consciences.
- Mary, quietly strengthening the disciples in the upper room when all seemed lost.
- Mary, Theotokos, the mother of God, mother of us wayward disciples, leading us along the way of peace.

A consistent and chastening teaching of the Church is that faith is a gift. It may be aided by our intellect, or our intellect may smooth out the contradictions, or our intellect may show

how appropriate such a belief is, but that last movement, that last leap of faith is in the dark. The grace for that ongoing journey is a gift—a gift we should constantly pray for. Lord, I believe, help my unbelief.

[13]

Suffering

By His Wounds We Are Healed

The Suffering Servant

Great suffering has marked life in Negros for many years. Not just the grinding suffering of the haciendas but also the suffering caused by the ongoing revolution. Many massacres come to mind, the Escalante massacre, the Langoni massacre, the Alingao massacre, the De los Santos massacre, the Magsungay massacre. Then there are the cases of torture, well documented, and the children caught in the crossfire or dying as a result of forced evacuations—hundreds of them. Who can ever fathom the anguish of their mothers? Negros is a land of suffering.

Where do we go to understand this terrible suffering of countless innocent victims—not just in Negros but throughout the world and more than ever in these times? A group of obscure passages, deep in the book of the prophet Isaiah—not by him, but by an unknown author—are the source of the Church's groping understanding of the mystery of suffering. These passages are collectively known as the songs of the suffering servant.

Brendan Lovett in his book *On Earth as in Heaven* explains how the songs of the suffering servant are a breakthrough, a "new vision" in human understanding of the mystery of life and suffering:

> The servant refuses to meet evil with evil. The servant does the unthinkable thing. He shows that the way forward is for the people to take on their own shoulders the burden of historical evil and creatively turn it around. . . . People come to recognize in this story of representative suffering the longed for dynamics of their own healing. . . . But despite this recognition of the truth of the song, they remained songs. There was somehow a shortage of singers. But Jesus took up that song and disciples of Jesus gropingly followed him into the darkness of this mystery by taking meaningless obscene and blasphemous suffering and using it to turn back the tide of evil and sorrow.[1]

But is there not the danger that in rehabilitating the redemptive power of suffering we will bolster in some way that passivity, which in a place like Negros sees suffering as the will of God and does nothing to remove its causes?

There is that danger, and the further danger that once again those who have for generations manipulated religion — any religion will do — to hold on to their structural domination will remind the poor callously that their sufferings will bring good. That is why it is necessary to remind people that suffering in itself is *not* good. It is evil. What the songs are saying is that all suffering can become redemptive and that that extra suffering the poor endure, precisely because they have stood up for their rights, has a special redemptive quality.

Daniel Berrigan, commentating on the same passage as Lovett, says that the suffering servant offers us a challenge: "Seek justice all the days of one's life and take the heat, the consequences."[2] And this, of course, was precisely what *the* Suffering Servant, Christ, did. He clearly sided with the poor to such an extent that the authorities set out specifically to discredit him, and eventually they arrested him, tortured him and executed him. This suffering, a paradigm for Christians, was the consequence of Jesus' activity for justice and for life.

The Song

But suffering takes different forms. Young Christians are often high on the more dramatic images of suffering. But suffering frequently turns out to be different from what we expected. For example: patience. For those dedicated to seeking justice and building peace, patience is one of the main sorts of suffering they will be called to endure: patience with those who do not see, patience with those who will not see, patience with the brethren so slow to come along, patience with ourselves when we do not match up to our own expectations. Patience comes from the Latin word *pati*, "to suffer."

The Prayer of Peace attributed to St. Francis has some beautiful lines that tell us of the suffering a peace-builder should expect.

> O Divine Master,
> grant that I may not so much seek
> to be consoled, as to console;
> to be understood, as to understand;
> to be loved, as to love;
> for it is in giving that we receive,
> it is in pardoning that we are pardoned,
> it is in dying (to self) that we are born
> to eternal life.

The challenge to see suffering in a redemptive light was strengthened from an unlikely source.

Benigno Aquino, Jr., was, in Filipino journalese, a Trapo: a traditional wheeler-dealer, no-deep-principles, party-hopping politician. However, he spent seven years in prison under Marcos, part of that in solitary confinement. During those dark hours his childhood faith nourished him, developed and led him to a deep conversion. He came to see that there was something more valuable than winning power. He even came to see that some are called to redeem the times. When he set out from Boston to return to Manila against the wishes of Marcos he knew he was taking his life in his hands and that losing his life was not the ultimate evil. When he was shot down descending the stairs of the plane, and when his body crashed onto the tarmac, his action awoke a whole generation and stirred the sort of idealism which helped to make the overthrow of Marcos possible at Edsa.

For a brief moment he had sung, however falteringly, the song of the suffering servant.

[14]

Common Sense

Fr. John Blowick

As a young seminarian I used to feel annoyed when Fr. John Blowick (co-founder of the Columban Fathers) talked so much about common sense. I felt in some way it was a code word for reneging on idealism. We should make sacrifices, but common sense said we should not go too far. We should give our lives, but common sense said we should hold something back.

It's been a quarter of a century or more, and I see the point now. Justice issues can be heady stuff. Not infrequently people will take up what is a relatively minor point of justice, clear-cut and logical — always logical — and pursue it relentlessly to a point of great bitterness and breakdown in their own community relationships. The issue in question happens to be a mere speck compared with the major issues of mass hunger and poverty the community should be facing, but the community has now been fractured seriously over the minor issue and is in no condition to face these major issues.

In a small town in the west of Ireland, a young enthusiastic labor leader brought the workers out on strike over a relatively minor grievance — the factory closed down leaving three hundred families affected. The labor leader shifted to another factory in the town, where he was soon elected head of the union. He brought all the workers out on another minor issue and again

177

closed the factory. Large numbers had to emigrate. The young man was proud of having stood for a principle.

In matters of peace-building there are only few instances where there is no room for flexibility and the humility of compromise if all the factors are taken into account. There is such a thing as genuine gradualism. But there is a type of character who gets the justice bit between his teeth and can't let go under any circumstances. His own "integrity" becomes more important than the lives of hundreds of people. This narrow reading of a situation is not unlike the fundamentalists' reading of the scriptures, verse by verse, rather than chapter by chapter, and that within the context and purpose of the whole book.

Such a person sometimes reminds us all that justice begins at home. If we do not have it here and now, how can we work for it outside? True, of course, justice does begin at home, but even within our homes, our real and spiritual families, we have to have patience and accept many defects. A relentless crusade against every inconsistency would destroy the very unity on which the power of the group to change injustice rests. True, the aim is logical from beginning to end, but its destructive results will far outweigh any virtue of justice.

So we must be able to distinguish between an inconsistency which can be lived with and inconsistency which poisons the heart of everything we do. I know no better phrase for the power or virtue of so distinguishing than *common sense*. The extra power and the punch contained in our opposition to injustice when we are united is close to magic, but that unity costs something and the price is that at times we have to see our own personal rights infringed and our just plans delayed. Recognizing the point where genuine integrity ends and servile compromise begins needs that elusive virtue—common sense. It is a sort of gift. Not everyone has it; I certainly do not claim to have it. But I can recognize it in others, and I can consult them, and I do.

Courage versus Cowardice

It sometimes happens that a moral question is reduced to a question of courage versus cowardice. We priests, in the first days of the Marcos regime, would sit around at night having beers and discussing the new situation. Many of our young friends had taken the decision to go into the mountains where they lived a very austere life, sleeping in the forest at night, hiding by day, living on roots. Someone would ask, "I wonder if I would have the courage to do that?" The conversation would center on the courage needed to make that decision. I got the impression at times that two other questions were pushed to the background: 1) the morality of the decision; and 2) the common sense of the decision. It is conceivable that such a decision would be morally correct. Some of our older confreres took a somewhat similar decision when the Japanese came to the Island of Mindanao in the southern Philippines; they went to the hills with the people and sometimes became chaplains to the *guerilleros* (as in the case of Monsignor Antonio Frondosa, later bishop of nearby Capiz). So, granting for the sake of argument that the decision itself is moral (don't forget the official Church approves the use of arms under certain conditions), does the decision pass the bar of common sense? Speaking to one young priest who was weighing the pros and cons I said, "You know, in the lowlands, as head of a parish, you could do great things to wake the people up to the reality of the injustice going on around them and to mobilize them to do something about it—in fact you can do that better than most lay people. In the mountains you are going to do something you have no training for and which most lay people can do better than you."

Not that courage is not an issue. Even as early as the time when St. Mark was writing his gospel, disciples were being tested and were having to show great courage: "You will be arrested and taken to court. You will be beaten in synagogues, and you will stand before Governors and Kings for my sake to be a witness before them" (Mark 13:9). When we get into peace-building, we will find that we will be in similar circumstances to those early Christians. We don't have to work in El Salvador or South Africa to get into danger. Behind the brazen main streets of most of the great cities of the world, people live under structured oppression. If we start lifting the lid on that, we will certainly be in danger.

So courage is needed and all the community support we can get is needed. We may have to wait for that support. And normally, we will have to work hard for it, and it will make a great difference in the effect on our work. I am not denying that, at times, we may just have to forge ahead on our own; it is common sense that will help us decide.

The decision made by various religious groups in the United States to hide political immigrants in their institutions—the Sanctuary movement—has been a courageous decision. It needed tedious and sometimes exasperating dialogue within each community, but it has led to more unity than division.

Hierarchy of Issues

In working for justice there is an interweaving of fear, courage and what used to be called human respect. What will people think of me? Common sense should not be lost sight of in the middle of these emotions, and normally a cooling off period and consultations with others will help to clarify the issue. Sometimes there is one pivotal issue which, in spite of it being pivotal, nevertheless gets obscured amid the others.

Once, while buying a jeep for mountain use, I checked and rechecked all the important requirements for a vehicle in the mountains: price, gasoline versus diesel, how many passengers, suspension and so on. I knew that the particular jeep model I was buying had a certain clearance from the ground that would be all right for the mountain roads. But I did not check it personally. So when I bought the vehicle, I discovered it was in fact too low. The metal body of the new model was heavier than the old, and that caused it to be a couple of vital inches closer to the ground, and that was not reflected in the official specifications. I had not checked that. All the other issues were of no consequence compared to that. The vehicle could not be driven in the mountains, and the question of whether I was using gasoline or diesel was now irrelevant. If I had kept that before my eyes, top of the list, I would not have ended up buying the wrong vehicle. The fact is, there is a hierarchy in issues.

We have limited physical energy, emotional energy and resources, so we must set priorities. We must decide what comes first, what is the central issue, the heart of the matter, and what good things therefore *must remain undone.* Common sense is surely needed here.

Sincerity

A justice issue may well be complicated. It is not simplified by the intense sincerity of the parties involved.

Who of us can fail to be impressed by sincerity? I recall a group of cadres of the New Peoples Army coming to my *convento* by night — this group was composed of leaders — quiet, soft-spoken, careful listeners. They had given up voluntarily a good standard of living to live in the mountains where they were hunted, traveling in their bare feet and eating the rice and dried fish of the people — but sometimes reduced to roots. I describe them at their best. The sincerity of such a group made a deep impression on me as a priest.

But the issue was never sincerity; in fact, sincerity may even cloud the issue. The issue was the rightness of the goal we worked for and the need to have a *means* to this goal which was *not intrinsically inimical to the goal itself.* It was my belief that part of that goal was a land of moderate equality where children no longer went hungry and people had a chance to better themselves because the economic structures were not totally loaded against them. Such a goal was not shared by the military I met. Their goal was to defeat the New Peoples Army and return the island to the way it always was — a land of silent plantations. The New Peoples Army's stated goal more closely approximated ours, though not completely and, of course, the NPA had a more detailed, more rigid picture of the end product.

We also differed from the New Peoples Army (and a fortiori with the military) on the means for attaining our goal. If life were seen as the highest value, and relationships among the living the cream on that dish, then taking lives deliberately was intrinsically at variance with our goal. We felt this was a gospel value which could not be compromised. The point being made here is that the sincerity of either side is not the issue. Sincerity in any cause is necessary, but sincerity is not enough. Who was it who ironically said, "How could we be wrong, when we were so sincere"?

The stakes are very high in the work for justice, and the language we use can be very heavy—life, death, genocide, massacre, oppression, starvation, torture of children. Suddenly it seems we must act now—immediately. And indeed that might be true, but the way is strewn with Christians who have given up all works of justice and maybe even the path of discipleship because they were not prepared to stay a while with the anguish and do the hard groundwork for some sort of consensus solution involving their companions. They wanted to do it all *now*.

The old word, I suppose, for common sense was prudence, but so often prudence was used as an excuse for avoiding an issue, for doing nothing, even for cowardice, that prudence has had a bad press. We need not worry about the over-prudent ones; we can hang onto common sense. As Pascal reminds us, the heart has its reasons that reason knows not of.

[15]

Spirituality in a Revolutionary Situation

Some of the readers of this book may be living in a revolutionary situation, a situation in which many people have decided that the conditions for a just revolution are present and have actually taken up arms. The decision to live a life of active nonviolence in these surroundings offers particular difficulties and calls for a particular spirituality. A sound spirituality must be based on a sound theology. That is why I have taken the time in the earlier chapters to show the basic theological grounds of that assertive form of peace-building known as active nonviolence.

But the theological groundwork is one thing; the way we live it out is another. The way we live it out is the spirituality.

In the popular mind spirituality is often reduced to particular prayer forms and devotions. These indeed reflect and strengthen a particular spirituality. But all spirituality, no matter what particular prayer form is used, *must relate to people*, because Christianity is about relationships. Christianity is a way of life. It is a journey made *with* others. Our relationships with others are paramount.

There are different spiritualities to suit different ways of life, and there are different devotions to suit these ways of life, but there is one nonnegotiable common denominator: all spirituality

is about our *relationships*, our "right relationships" with the different groups we interact with. If this is present, then the resulting sense of God's presence we feel is authentic. If this is absent, no matter how high the spiritual euphoria, it is bogus. And this holds true for solitary contemplation.

In Negros five groups offer a special challenge for those of us working for peace: the poor, the rich, the revolutionaries, the military and our own co-workers.

The situation in Negros will differ from that in Harlem, or South Africa or Paraguay, but there will be similarities which, with proper adaptation, will help the reader focus the problems in his or her particular situation and, anyway, the underlying principles will be the same.

The Poor

Our relationship with the poor tends to be patronizing. We help them. After a while we realize we should be helping them to help themselves. So far so good, but we must take a further step — we must accept the difficult truth that the poor have much to teach us. This has been the great insight resulting from our coming closer to them. And it begins the moment we stop patronizing them and start to respect them as persons.

I recall a strange meeting many years ago, though I cannot recall why I should have been present. The government had decreed that each sack of sugar would be taxed and that money would go to the "upliftment" of the workers. A powerful sugar planter, who had undergone a conversion at the Cursillo, called a meeting to discuss how this money — the Amelioration Fund — would be spent. I was at that meeting and so was Fr. Luis Jalandoni. I was impressed that these sugar planters were proposing that some of the Amelioration Fund should be spent on spiritual retreats for the workers. That seemed good to me and praiseworthy. The group members were excited and happy with themselves that we were thinking up something so creative and religious. All this time Fr. Luis Jalandoni remained quiet.

Finally, he spoke: "Have the workers been consulted?" There was silence. The answer was obviously no. "It is, after all, their money"—his voice and eyes could not now conceal his anger. Suddenly I realized with embarrassment that I had fully accepted the unsaid wisdom: We will be the ones to speak for the poor.

That movement from patronizing the poor, working for the poor to working with the poor, results in a *new relationship* with them, a relationship in which we respect them as persons, as individuals, as having a dignity that we would want people to respect in ourselves. This new relationship means we can begin to listen to the poor, maybe for the first time, and so learn from them. Learn what?

Family love was one thing I saw. They would mortgage the last water buffalo or bit of land to pay for a sick member of the family. Many of the people who lived in the mountains where I lived lost their land precisely in this way. For them, people were more important than things.

Another thing I learned from many of them was the extraordinary sense of the presence of God in the working out of the strands of life. It seemed to give them power to endure great hardship, which in their circumstances was unavoidable.

One of the places we meet the poor is in prison. In our stay in prison mentioned above, our superior, Fr. Michael Martin, used to say to us, "Remember, you are in here to learn." Now this was a very grim prison. If you have seen the film "The Kiss of the Spider Woman," you have an idea of it. It was like living in holes in the ground—no toilets, no running water, no furniture of any sort in most of the cells. I used to say, "Learn from the prisoners? I don't hear the prisoners teaching me any deep theological truths. All the prisoners are saying here is *Diin ang imo kalooy?*—'Where is your holy pity?'—help us." And that angered me. Because I had reached that stage where I felt handing them money would demean them and me and alter our relationship.

But someone had sent into the prison Albert Nolan's book *Jesus Before Christianity.*[1] Nolan emphasizes the compassion

Jesus had for the poor. Compassion was his faith put into practice. Compassion and faith were in some respects practically one and the same thing. Suddenly I realized that the prisoners were not asking for pity. They were saying: "Where is your compassion? Don't you see that our teeth are falling out, that we have no clothes, that we have no meat to eat except rats. You can get a little bit of something with your connections. Share some of it. We're your brothers. Can't you *see* that we're your brothers?" That's what they were saying. And after all, that is the heart of the good news.

So, at the center of a spirituality to be lived out in a revolutionary situation is the discipline of learning from the poor, letting them teach us. But they teach us not just because of their human wisdom, but precisely because they are sorely oppressed and our God, as the psalms and prophets and Exodus tell us again and again, is the God of the oppressed. He comes to them in a special way. He hears their cry. When we touch the poor, we touch God in some way.

God is the God of life. Where people are crying out for life, God is there. And if we are there, we will encounter God in ways beyond our comprehension.

However, the poor have the temptation of abusing the theology of "the will of God." They tend to accept their fate, to be fatalistic. They lose interest in striving. They don't see that activity to change their situation is a sacred call of God and a means of sanctification. The antidote to this turned out to be better Basic Christian Communities.

Through the Base Communities we learned that in struggling to change our situation, we grow as human beings. We learned that getting what we are struggling for may not be the most important thing. We may not get what we're after. *But getting it isn't as important as the act of struggling for it.*

What if we want to regain a piece of land taken unjustly and the mayor walks in and says, "You can have it?" All we get is the land. But if we work nonviolently together, struggling, growing in confidence, growing in fellowship—the land we win is nothing compared to what we have gained as human beings. The land is important, but even more important is becoming human beings—through the purifying process of struggle.

Growing in self-reliance, growing in a sense of self-worth, growing in the ability to say no to those who would have us cooperate in our own destruction—these are real values which we learn to appreciate when we work with the poor. In a prolonged nonviolent struggle we learn not to look too immediately for physical results like new buildings.

This doesn't mean we shouldn't look for results. We should. We should be struggling to change things. There is no way we should stop. But we know that it is the struggle itself which makes us grow and that growth is our main aim. It is a wonderful thing to see people who had no sense of self-worth grow in front of your eyes. Some people in the Philippines call this the theology of struggle.

Another point I have learned: never refuse to accept the gifts of the poor. It is sometimes hard to accept these gifts. We say to ourselves, "They have nothing; I have everything." But they are not just giving a gift, they are giving their dignity, their love. We must bow our head and say a sincere thank you for those eggs, for example, knowing she is giving more than all the gifts we've ever given.

There is a danger that when we discover the riches of the poor we will fall head over heels; the poor can do no wrong; we canonize them. This is a dangerous delusion; the poor are as human as anyone else, and as liable to betray, to double-cross, to let us down. Then many people get disillusioned and turn against the poor. What we need is a new and heightened sensitivity to the sacramentality of the poor, but this sensitivity must have its feet firmly on the ground.

The Rich

Many of the rich *use* religion; they separate it from their business lives, they keep religion to Sunday and charities. Whether consciously or unconsciously, they keep the poor where they are. They tend to think that things are more important than people, unless the people are their own family. Then, frequently, they spoil them silly till they are dull, obnoxious, overfed polyps. Directly or indirectly, they keep the poor in poverty. Part of the way they do it is through the Church, where the building often becomes more important than the people who worship within its walls. The rich are often quite willing to pay for church buildings.

Priests and nuns, and especially bishops albeit unconsciously, are a special target of the rich. Certain business people see the value of having a clerical collar on their committee. They see it far more than we see it. A nun, a priest—best of all, a bishop.

One Negros priest used to give a mordant parable: It was his parable of the prostitute. "As a prostitute is pampered and provided for, so she is fully compliant. Sometimes in the same spirit, a priest in Negros is offered gifts both for himself and for his church, provided he continues to bless the status quo and remains silent on issues of wages, military operations and human rights. Then there is the classy prostitute. Her favors are sought by the very rich. They dance attention upon her—flowers, food, and a Mercedes at the door. Just watch the antics of some people at the bishop's palace."

When I am with the rich, I have to take care not to be prostituted, but I also have to take care not to despise them. It is very tempting to write off all that they do, to consider it all hypocrisy. It isn't all hypocrisy. But we have to refuse their large gifts.

I think of some wealthy people I knew. They lived not far from a farming cooperative I had started. They were quite hardworking people themselves. I dropped in on them one day. The man of the house asked me right away if I needed a jeep! I said I didn't. "All you have to do is ask," he said. And at that moment I very nearly asked. It was only my guardian angel who kept the words in my mouth. Then he asked how I liked the whiskey we were drinking. I said it was great. "Well, Father, we have a bottle for you to take home." And before I got out of the house I had that bottle of whiskey and two packs of cigarettes and a new cigarette lighter — and I was feeling terrible. A few days later I met his brother-in-law. He told me he was running for election and would be grateful for any assistance I could give. "With all these Christian Communities you must have a lot of influence, Father, and you know I am working for the 'little people.' "

And the rich can change. All right, not so often. But with God all things are possible. Zacchaeus and Nicodemus changed. One time Luis Jalandoni had a face-to-face showdown with a powerful landlord. It ended up with a public slanging match, unusual in Philippine culture. The *hacendero* called Luis names and Luis kept answering "the same to you." Most unlike Luis.

Twenty years later I was giving a talk on social matters and to my amazement I saw him, the *hacendero*, up in the front seat. I resented him being there, and I said to myself someone has invited him here to ask a donation from him (not far from the truth). My talk was quite strong, though I felt uncomfortable with him in the front row looking at me. It was not the sort of talk I'd expect him to be at, knowing him.

After the talk he approached me and congratulated me. I took this to be the normal obligatory congratulation given to a speaker coming down from the dais. In the Philippines not to shake his or her hand in congratulation would be ill mannered. However, he repeated his remark and said further that he personally agreed with everything I had said, and he asked to talk to me. I was wary.

"Do you mind if I sit down, Padre? I'm getting old now. I'm seventy-six, and I need a walking stick, as you can see. You know I have a large sugar farm. I inherited it from my mother, and she inherited it from her father. I have, apart from the sugar cane, eight hundred mango trees. Each tree produces about two thousand mangoes a year, and you know the price of mangoes now. I have ten thousand coconut trees. My wife and I planted all those trees when we were newly married many years ago. The coconuts and the mangoes must be worth more than a million a year, not to mention the sugar. Padre, I have decided to give it all to the workers."

Then he explained his proposal. He wasn't just going to divide it up. He planned a program of education and support and a process by which they (the workers) would buy it gradually. This was not a ploy to give it and then not give it; to give with one hand and take back with the other. He realized that the workers would drown under the weight of such a gift, so it needed careful planning. He finished by saying, "I don't need all this work [referring to the complex plan of giving them the land] at my age. I'd rather rest. And I've gotten little help from the Department of Agrarian Reform. They don't seem to know their ass from their elbow. And they are so completely mired in bureaucracy. But this way is the only way to make it work."

I thought of all our failed efforts to get anything across to the *hacenderos* this last twenty years. "The light shines in the darkness and the darkness does not overcome it."

The Military

In Negros, frequently the soldiers in the field are nothing more than thugs handed a gun, given the first bit of power they ever got in their lives and determined to use it especially against the poor. They have a cringing respect for the rich, who have access to their officers and will be able to complain. And apart from that, the basic feudal culture tells them that they, the troops, had better respect the rich.

As for the officer class, they have frequently been destroyed by the years of the Marcos regime. The old idealism is gone; they have been given a taste of power and are not going to give it up. The sang-froid with which they lie is now legendary, as those of us who have traipsed from military camp to military camp looking for missing people know. Many have been trained in torture techniques, as the McCoy interviews[2] reveal, and as a result have a chilling ruthlessness.

In dealing with the military, I have to remind myself of these principles:

First, we are working to bring about the Kingdom, the Kingdom begins here, and in that Kingdom we are all brothers and sisters. In God's plan, these men are my brothers.

Second, these military men have a heart and a conscience however much they have been hardened in battle and indoctrinated and even intoxicated by anti-communist ideology. They are not all the same.[3] When I mentally label them "the enemy," I dehumanize them and, in the process, dehumanize myself.

Third, they are professional liars. It is unrealistic to ignore this fact. While leaving open the possibility that what they say might be true, I must never believe it without checking. I have been a victim myself of their lies and have seen how they have consistently and effectively in certain quarters vilified the character of Bishop Fortich. In wartime words are weapons.

Fourth, historically the armed forces of the Philippines have produced great bravery among the soldiers. Many stories from the Second World War bear this out, not least the Death March to Bataan. Even in recent years many cases of bravery beyond the call of duty have been recorded. Also, among the soldiers and officers there are some who want to change the Philippines to a better place and do have genuine compassion for the poor.

Fifth, when all the analysis is over and done, members of the military are Filipinos, with many of the positive cultural values of the Philippines: an innate respect for the old and for women, an innate respect for cultural religion in spite of the indoctrination which indicts any religious person in favor of social reform as communist.

It is sometimes possible to get through to them using a cultural approach. Many a time when people had disappeared and we had failed to get anything but lies out of the commanders, the soldiers lower down, when approached by a mother or a grandmother, would admit that, yes, the young man in question was inside the barracks. They would even let the women in to see the boy if enough tears were shed. (This was vital because identifying the place of detention was one of the greatest safeguards against the person being "salvaged"—taken out in the night, killed and dumped far away.)

There is no doubt that the respect of the ordinary men in the army for the cultural religious symbols of the statue of the Virgin

Mary, the Infant Jesus and for the Sisters in traditional garb played a major part in stopping the Marcos tanks in the 1986 February revolution in Manila.

However that may be, a major problem in dealing with the military is that they are trained to obey without asking questions.

We were under detention for a month in a military camp. The colonel had given us a room right in the bustling center of military activities. We were quite shocked to see how officers reported, listened carefully, clicked their heels, tipped their cap and said, "Yes, Sir."

We met during this time with our religious superiors and discussed the issues. We began to contrast our own wrestling with the question "What is the right thing to do?" with that of the military, for whom the name of the game seemed to be "Yes, Sir." The disciple must know the moral implication of an action. Surely the military obedience and the disciples' obedience are poles apart. So there will be an inevitable clash. In the early Church it was inconceivable to be a soldier and a disciple at the same time. *Christianus sum, non possum militari*, "I am a Christian; I cannot become a soldier," said St. Justin Martyr.

As a result, every now and again a disciple will be called to confront the military and in plain language say, "What you are doing is wrong," and take the consequences. Fortich was always one to avoid confrontation, but when it came to the forced military evacuations of 1989, when the military in Negros forced some thirty thousand people to evacuate the mountains, Fortich condemned the action outright. It was one of Fortich's last acts as Bishop of Bacolod, and it earned him undying hatred.

Hundreds of children died in that operation—Operation Thunderbolt. We heard not one word of protest from the many army chaplains. Some day the Church is going to have to reexamine the whole morality of the role of such chaplains. What spiritual value have they if they are not going to comment on the moral dimension of military activity?

As I write I must admit I feel anger surging up in me. Anger may be distasteful, but it is not wrong. It is a natural human reaction on seeing an injustice—or a perceived injustice.

What must be avoided here is hate. Some people working for peace and justice reach the stage where they cannot look on a man in uniform without hatred. But, is not our point of disagreement with the military precisely their lack of respect for other human beings, who we claim are our brothers and sisters? To surrender to hate would be to undermine the whole purpose of our endeavor, which is to initiate that Kingdom where people live in mutual respect and love.

The content of Jesus' teaching differs in one respect from the great religious teachers before him, that is, his teaching to love our enemies. He does not say we should not have enemies. In fact, he implies we will have them if we follow him. But he does say to "Love your enemies, do good to those who hate you. Bless those who curse you and pray for those who treat you badly" (Luke 6:27b-28).

The Revolutionaries

Another group we must relate to are the revolutionaries. Revolutions and revolutionaries differ enormously from country to country. I speak here only of the Island of Negros. And I speak of relating as people who have made a core decision for non-violence relating with people who have the same desire for peace and justice but who believe that armed struggle is the only way forward in this case. The relating is complicated further if some of the revolutionaries, in the Marxist tradition, see religion as an obstacle.

As I look back on my own contacts, so many faces pass before my memory. I think of Boy, the husband of Virgie. Boy was one of the most gentle people I ever knew. I certainly knew myself to be a more violent person than he. But he left the seminary to join the revolution. He married Virgie. They invited me to do the wedding—I couldn't go. I think I saw Boy only once after that before he was killed, leaving Virgie with their only son. Many years have passed. Virgie still works away quietly, a life of hardship and dedication in the cause that Boy died for. It is with respect and trepidation I talk about people like this.

How then to relate to such revolutionaries? For me, it is very important to respect their views. After all, these views basically rested on the just-war or just-revolution theory, which though I have trouble accepting it, is nevertheless still the official teaching of the Church. In this respect, ironically, they could be said to be more Catholic than I.

My attitude was and is that a Christian must be prepared to dialogue across barriers like these in spite of the difficulties. Someday the pain and anguish will bear fruit. The immediate effect, of course, was to give some people ammunition for suspecting us of "being in cahoots with the communists."

Again and again we were accused: "Father, you don't realize but you are being used by the communists." This was because we protested, for example, the evacuations. My answer was that the Church has been shamelessly used by right-wing groups for generations, and now some people are suddenly worried about it being used by left-wing groups. I agree strongly we should not allow ourselves to be "used," but we should not refuse to take up an issue *solely* because another group has also taken it up. And there are things a disciple of nonviolence can learn from the revolutionaries. No one could fail to be moved by the obvious dedication of so many of them, by their lives of frugality, hardship and sincerity. Surely I could learn from this frugality and simplicity of lifestyle. And the sincerity? Sincerity is not enough, was never enough, and it is no guarantee against being wrong. But it can be so refreshing when seen beside the duplicity, opportunism and total lack of principles of the traditional politicians, who see the political scene as an enormous cockfight. Their sole aim is to bet on the winning bird.

What a contrast with the readiness of so many of the revolutionaries to die for their cause. The islands of the Philippines are strewn with the graves of hundreds of them, who left comfortable homes and faced death and often torture. It is incorrect, however, to apply Christ's words about giving one's life for one's friend to either the military or the revolutionaries. Those words of Christ refer specifically to giving one's life *while deliberately refusing to take life.* The war memorials have it wrong.

Apart from learning from the revolutionaries, we should also be true to our own vision and challenge them. Anything less would do them a disfavor. However, we only have a right to challenge them to the degree that we have condemned the violence against which they have taken up arms. Too many people leap in with condemnations of people of violence, when these same people have remained silent about the injustices, the inequalities, the racial and religious discrimination which are major causes of the armed response.

Though it is true that revolutionaries tend to be rigid and ideological (in the negative sense of that word), and that this can lead them to be closed and to have no room for new information, or to lose sight of ordinary human values, or even to be involved in atrocities.[4] Nevertheless they have no monopoly on these attitudes; they are an occupational hazard for any of us who are deeply committed to a cause. Nor have they a monopoly on ideology; all of us who hope to apply our vision to the concrete situation develop an ideological framework, but that framework should serve our vision, not warp or maim it or indeed warp or maim us. As Bertolt Brecht warned:

> Even the hatred of squalor makes the brow grow stern,
> even anger against injustice makes the voice grow harsh.
> Alas, we who wished to lay the foundation of kindness
> could not ourselves be kind.[5]

The revolutionaries in Negros rely on careful Marxist analysis to expose the causes of injustice and the hidden motives of social groups. They rely on a renewed sense of their own dignity and power to change things. All this does not sit easily with belief in the power of prayer and religion, because superficially it seems to pit scientific analysis against religion. It needs some thinking through. So some of them will see prayer as a waste of time and the Christian Communities as merely a useful front. Others have preserved their faith strongly; in fact their faith was the starting point of their involvement. One of them told me how, as a boy, in a large poor family with a father who beat him and his mother, it was his mother who had kept the whole family together. He knew her source of strength was her rising in the morning at 4:30 and praying quietly before their little altar. It was memories like this that inspired him and other fellow cadres to insist on the freedom to choose. His group won the day, and the Negros revolutionaries had a more open outlook on religion than those in some other areas.

A particular problem arose when people who once worked with us decided to join the revolution, but still kept working legally. With regard to joining the revolution, we understood their decision, but we used to say to them: "Don't try working the two things together, the legal and the illegal, because you will drag the legal group you are working with into suspicion and damage their good work and might even put them in danger. Your presence gives the military the opportunity to call the whole legal group communists and make any member fair game for salvaging."

The labor union is a case in point. All of us decry the leaders of the yellow union, who sell out their workers and make a sweetheart contract with management. By the same token it would be wrong for union leaders to use the union merely as an adjunct to armed struggle. Members have joined in the name of the stated principles of unionism which are specifically democratic and nonviolent. They will find themselves intimidated, terrorized and suppressed (God knows they suffer those things anyway) to a now unbearable degree if some of their leaders have secretly taken them where they did not opt to go. Such union leaders need to ask themselves if they are being honest with the laborers and if they will not ultimately cripple the desperately needed union movement—to the delight of plantation owners.

What if a member of a religious order decides to join the armed struggle? That poses a real dilemma for persons vowed to a very special relationship with the members of their community. They now must hold secrets from the community, but what to one person is a vital secret to another appears as deceit.

Deep hurt results from this, but then many young religious feel as bound in conscience to join the revolution as their confreres feel bound not to. Wisdom is needed here as one picks a way between Eastern flexibility and Western logic. A time may come, however, when integrity demands that they make a clear choice between the two ways of life.

Relating with the revolutionaries in our midst in a time of war is fraught with danger from every direction, but as disciples do we have any choice? Ched Myers in *Binding the Strong Man: A Political Reading of Mark's Story of Jesus*[6] shows us the Marcan community between the years 67 and 70 in a situation very akin to that of the Christian Communities of Negros. This community was caught between the Roman imperial oppressors and the determined Zealot nationalist revolutionaries. The Marcan community chose the difficult path of staunch opposition to the oppressive invaders coupled with a determination to use only those means their Master had used. In that context the saying of Mark's Jesus, "Take up your cross and follow me," was not a poetic counsel to asceticism but a grim call to oppose injustice even if it meant being executed by crucifixion along with the Zealots.

Writing these pages has been difficult. What dialogue can there be between two strongly held conflicting views — and yet the fact that both of us want a new world is surely a starting point. When all is said and done, we have been talking of "means." The revolutionaries have the advantage that they clearly name their means — armed struggle — and that they put their lives on the line to prove their sincerity. We, on the other hand, are only discovering our means and are not exposed to the same risks as they are. And we are not fully backed by our Church, to whom we look for guidance and strength. Ironically, our Church has difficulty in accepting the example of our Founder in putting aside the sword; she looks back over her shoulder all the time to the Old Testament. In this ambivalence she takes the ground from under her protestations of the absolute value of human life even in the womb. She is seen to have two standards and her witness "for life" is fragmented.

The day we can present a Church whose stated passion for justice is backed by a passion for life which condemns *all* killing, that day we will be able to offer, with credibility, to our revolutionary brothers and sisters an option which is more radical than they ever dreamed of.

Our Co-workers

I don't know why it should be, but my experience is that those of us involved in justice and peace work suffer more from burnout than any other group. The disturbing thing is that after the burnout many of us never return to any work for peace. Is it something like a person who has a literalist approach to the Bible and then when this faith is shattered he or she moves to disbelief or indifference? I ask this because so many good people have moved, as it were, from all to nothing. That explains my own fear (too much fear?) for those who take a rigidly ideological stand. I fear we're going to lose them. Their going is a loss. The Christian community needs them and misses them.

Apart from frequent burnout, there is a great deal of anguish, tension and friction going with peace-building in a revolutionary situation. We do need a special spirituality.

One of the particular agonies we face is that of trying to discern the limits, the boundaries of our cooperation with other groups whose aims are only partly the same as our own.

I recall being approached on two occasions by the NPA to borrow my jeep. The first was when they had some people in trouble. I did not fully understand the circumstances, but I feared in some way I could be aiding an ambush, so I refused. Later I worried that I had refused to help to save some lives. In real life situations you don't always have all the facts.

On the second occasion two young NPAs – brothers – had received word that their father was dying; they wanted to get his last blessing. Would I lend them the jeep? This time I did.

A nurse friend of mine who ran the village health program has continuously been faced with being asked to attend sick and wounded NPAs. She took a serious risk in that, but she felt she could not refuse. On one occasion she attended a soldier and an NPA who had wounded each other in an encounter; neither knew she attended the other. Later the NPA defected to the military and was detailed by his captain to shoot the nurse. He did not carry out the order. Other doctors and medical people have not been so fortunate; being faithful to their Hippocratic oath cost them their lives.

When we priests signed the Collegial Statement against the mass evacuations, that was seen as oblique support for the NPA. Of course the NPA was probably delighted with our statement. I myself was not happy with every adjective in the statement, but I felt that the very stones would cry out if we did not speak.

What if you are asked to appear on a platform condemning torture and you find yourself standing beside someone with whose opinion you disagree strongly in some other matter? That may be no problem in times of peace, but where there is an undeclared war in progress everything is seen in terms of "for us or against us"; along with the shooting war goes the propaganda war. Even a call for peace may not be a sincere call for peace but an attempt to put the opponent on the wrong foot before the public. What should you do if your group is asked to join a prayer rally for peace under these circumstances?

There is no easy way out, no escape from the anguish. Sometimes we get it wrong. By its very nature a revolutionary situation is a time of turmoil. We are constantly pushed to make decisions on the hop. Sometimes it seems as if we are trying to cross a river jumping from moving log to moving log. The danger is that we could become so pragmatic that we fall into ways which ultimately tear us apart. I have put together here a few points and guidelines that could help us to keep the peace among ourselves in the midst of the fray:

> 1. Know your own principles and be able to distinguish the substance from the appearances; a well-ordered discussion can help to clarify these during a time of confusion.

2. If you have a clear stand and your integrity is known and accepted, then, in cases of doubt, you will be given the benefit of the doubt by the people who matter.

3. You are not going to get each individual step correct. You are judged over a period for a series of acts, not on a single individual act—except by fools or knaves.

4. You fear to lose a friend if you take a certain stand. If, after careful discernment, you see the stand is right and important, then take that stand. This will show you who your real friends are.

5. Some things like torture cry out for condemnation. If your condemnation causes scandal to some people, it is not because you give it but because they take it.

6. Courtesy is never wrong. Greeting an opponent does not mean you agree with the person. The grace of God is in courtesy.

7. Don't be politically naive; analyze the political backdrop to the action.

8. Don't let someone manipulate you by using your mutual friendship to pull you into doing something that has political implications with which you do not agree.

9. Ask advice from a disinterested wise third party; this seems elementary, but sometimes we forget.

10. There are times when a decision must be made on the spur of the moment, but normally don't be forced; ask for time and sleep on it. Sometimes the postponement of a decision is a way to extricate yourself from the straitjacket of a yes or no solution which is being pushed on you inopportunely.

11. So much misunderstanding can be avoided if we inform others of our actions beforehand. They may not agree, but at least they have the real story and not a wild rumor.

12. There are so many disagreements between and within peace groups over money, over funding. Follow the strictest public standards of accounting and transparency. If this is standard procedure, then no one will feel hurt and a lot of pain and disruption will be avoided.

13. Some people have that splendid gift of being able to disagree with you thoroughly on a serious matter and still show deep respect and even affection. We need to cultivate this gift with our co-workers.

14. Don't manipulate others. State clearly what you want and don't have a double agenda. Nothing is more calculated to undermine the harmony of the group. By double agenda, I mean that you ask them to do something for one reason but you actually have in mind a second purpose. In classic manipulation the second purpose is something they would not agree to if they knew about it beforehand. You have covered yourself logically and legally because of the first purpose, but if the matter is serious you can say goodbye to *trust* after that. And without mutual trust no peace movement can hold together.

15. Point out to others when they are manipulating you. Normally, sadly, it's friends who manipulate us and it's friends we manipulate, frequently without consciously adverting to it.

16. Manipulation totally undermines the friendship on which true cooperation is based.

17. A common form of manipulation is to ask friends for something at a time or place which makes it difficult to refuse. You have taken away their freedom. They may not notice it now, but a residue of ill will is inevitable. You have gained a point cheaply. There will be a price to pay later.

18. Don't use all your force on every issue; let some issues pass. Keep your powder dry for the more important issues. Knowing the difference, ah, there's the rub!

19. Don't be dismissive of others who are not as "advanced" as you. The word *advanced* can be presumptuous and even a touch arrogant. We need every bit of the Church's rich tradition in building the Kingdom of God and not everyone needs to be doing the same thing. "If the whole body were an eye where would be the hearing? If the whole body were an ear where would be the sense of smell?" (1 Cor. 12:7).

20. No one in the group has all the virtues, but the group as a whole should have.

21. Justice is not the only virtue; without joy and compassion justice can be cold and even vicious. ("If I give away all I have and deliver my body to be burned and have not love, I gain nothing.")

22. Read and ponder and pray the Beatitudes; they are the Magna Carta of Jesus' nonviolent way.

23. When does acceptable cooperation become unacceptable collaboration? The line between the two can be very thin. There is no pat formula, no escape from the anguish in trying to discern and no guarantee that we won't get it wrong. But we will get it right more often if we keep an eye to the above points.

Most of all, there is one central fact of faith so often forgotten by believers who are working for justice and peace that it needs repeating. The central fact of our faith is this: *Jesus is alive.* He has overcome death. He is here. He is now. Emmanuel, Christ is with us. Why do we stand here moaning? "For I believe neither death nor life nor Principalities nor Powers can separate us from the love that is in Christ Jesus." That Love is a Person. How about allowing him a chance to help — a chance to participate in building his kingdom?

[Epilogue]

Island of Hope

No Hope!

A few hundred yards from the airy apartment where I have been writing this book is a squatter area called Magsungay, a coastal slum where tattered shacks elbow each other along the sandy shoreline. Some of the residents have come from the plantations; others have fled from the shellings. All seek to avail of the "free" status of shoreline land. The Alvarado family are such people, though indeed they have been here now some twenty-five years.

When I came back to the Philippines I thought of living in Magsungay. We Columbans have a parish there and I had the idea of living close to the really poor. That was before I saw the place properly. When I actually toured around, I told myself I couldn't put an office there. But the truth is that my senses were so assaulted by the smells, the heat, the steaming refuse, the children playing in inky water, the flies in the open sewers, that my fine intentions melted away.

Aileen Alvarado and Noel Garcia were both born here in Magsungay; their parents are fisher folk. Aileen is curly headed and even featured, a shy Filipina beauty. Noel is black from long days at sea in his open boat. They grew up together here and were sweethearts from childhood. They have three children, Noelyn, Eddan, and little one-year-old Marylyn. They built their shack next to Aileen's parents' house, where the tide comes up even to your waist. That's why all the houses are on stilts.

Hardly an arrow's flight from these shoreline shacks are the discos and new hotels of Bacolod. Their lights blaze till the early hours and in the casino millions of pesos change hands each night. Aileen and Noel are hardly aware of this world as they sleep on the floor with their children cuddled in around them. Marylyn will only sleep in the arms of Noel. Their little house has not one stick of furniture, and neither here nor in the Alvarado's house is there ever more food than for one day. Yet Aileen and Noel are happy, they have each other and the security of knowing that Aileen's mother and father and two brothers are only yards away. This is their wealth, and they wish for no other.

However, for some time there had been a cloud on the horizon. A wealthy man in Manila, let's call him Mr. X, claims the land their houses are built on. This man is a millionaire, not only from his vast sugar property in Negros but his financial concerns in Manila and even in New York. Of course all this is legal and in the form of a family holding; if you try to approach it, you find yourself dealing with a faceless corporation. Anyway, this corporation does have a face in Negros in the person of an administrator, a powerful man in Bacolod. And he has one of the local police in his employ, Badong.

It is Badong's job to get the people off the land. However, like the publicans in the pay of the Roman authorities in Palestine, Badong seems to be making something on the side himself, unbeknownst to his employers. When new people arrive he doesn't prevent them; he just charges them. He could not charge the Alvarados or the Garcias because they know their rights, they have been here for twenty-five years and they know that some sort of court order would be necessary to get them off. Apart from that, the tide comes in here up to your waist. It's *littoral*, government land. The Alvarados and their likes pose a special problem for Badong, who with his uniform and gun can more easily intimidate the wretched new arrivals. For some time Badong has been giving verbal threats to the Alvarados, and he made an assault with an axe on Aileen and Noel's shack, forcing them to move in with their parents.

We were all recovering from typhoon Ruping, the most furious typhoon in memory. The cement walls around the compound where I live had been blown down. The house of the Alvarados had also been badly damaged, so they were rebuilding it, much to the annoyance of Badong, because traditionally after a typhoon or a fire is an ideal time to get squatters off, particularly by moving in fast with a temporary fence and guards while the dazed families are sheltering in the local school. But the Alvarados had not moved away and were now rebuilding their house with the help of the local barrio captain, Antonio Alisbo, who was a carpenter. The house was eight feet by twelve, the size of a one-car garage. The two Alvarado boys were wielding saws and hammers with the help of Antonio Alisbo and their father. Watching happily was their mother and their sister Aileen with her two older children. At rest inside the house while the hammering was going on was Noel with Marylyn asleep on his left arm. He had been at sea all night.

Though Noel had snoozed through the din, he was suddenly alerted by the new sound of the arrival of a motor bike and a jeep. The motor bike was Badong's; the jeep was the service vehicle of the local police and had on board one policeman and two vigilantes. Noel heard Badong's voice, "If you go ahead building that house, I'll break it down." Then he heard Aileen's brother answer, "You've broken down our sister's house, now you want to break down our parents' house."

That very afternoon, a Sunday, my neighbor was scything the grass around both our apartments when he heard firecrackers. I was asleep with an air conditioner on, so I heard nothing. But what my neighbor heard were not firecrackers, but round after round of shots from the M16 assault rifle of Badong as he mowed down the two old Alvarados, their two sons, and the barrio captain. Aileen threw herself over Noelyn and Eddan. Noel ducked down with Marylyn but felt two bullets enter his body. Marylyn jerked and blood began to ooze out from her little tummy and her entrails began to bulge out through the bullet holes. Noel tried to press them in with his hands. He called for help but Badong was now riding away on his motor bike. The jeep with the policeman and two vigilantes also left, leaving the ground covered with dead and dying.

Noel ignored the wounds in his arm and thigh and kept calling for help to get Marylyn to a hospital. The closest hospital was the Sanitarium; someone got a taxi and sped off with Marylyn while others took Noel to the free government hospital at the other side of the city. When the taxi with Marylyn arrived at the private hospital, the staff asked where the parents were. They would need their signatures. The man explained that there had been a massacre, could they not just operate? No, first there had to be a five-thousand peso down payment. They put Marylyn back in the taxi and set out for the other side of the city to the free government hospital. She was brought into the emergency room where she saw her father Noel lying on a stretcher. Though only a year old she recognized him immediately and began to cry, "Tatay, Tatay."

Noel was beside himself with anguish. From his stretcher he kept asking that they attend to Marylyn, but they needed to do an x-ray first. The x-ray showed three bullets in her stomach. By the time they operated it was too late. Marylyn died some hours later, bringing to six the number killed.

Ten thousand people marched in the silent funeral procession to the graveyard. There were no banners, no songs, no slogans, just silence and the low sound of weeping, crying out to heaven from this island of tears.[1]

Who says land is not a problem in Negros? A few days after being installed as president, Fidel Ramos appointed a Negros landlord as minister for Agrarian Reform and immediately proposed raising the maximum land retention to eight times higher than it had been under Marcos. As Tallyrand said about the Bourbon kings: "They have forgotten nothing and they have learned nothing!" As surely as there is a God in heaven, Negros will not be at peace till the elite accept that the peasants must have a reasonable human share in the wealth of this island. No wonder some people feel there is no hope.

And yet I do not agree. There may be no grounds for optimism, but there are grounds for hope, and that brings me to my last two stories.

Our Hope

I was driving home one night. It was a time when Bacolod
was filled with evacuees. As I passed near the Capitol I thought
I saw some figures lying on the cement sidewalk; unusual, as
there was no overhead protection at that point. I stopped and
went over to see if someone was sick. I was greeted by an old
woman. "No, don't worry, Sir. We're all right; we're just settling
down for the night." Beside her was a crude wooden cart, a
vegetable barrow on top as a sort of second story. A stirring and
a little human gurgle came from behind the sack which covered
the lower story. "Oh, that's my daughter and her baby." At that
moment the sack was pulled back from inside to reveal a young
woman stretched out with a baby in her arms. "You know, my
daughter was abandoned by her husband. Together we came
over the mountain to look for him, but we couldn't find him.
Now we support ourselves during the day selling vegetables from
our barrow and at night she sleeps in the barrow and I watch
here. A man came by here and began kissing the baby in a way
I didn't like. I stopped him. Was I right?" "Yes," I replied, "very
right." Eventually I said I'd be going along, but as I turned I
almost kicked over the embers of a dying fire. In its glow I caught
sight of what seemed to be two very old people asleep together
on the cement, covered only by some transparent plastic against
the night chill. "Who are these, Lola? (Grandmother)" I asked;
I was half alarmed. "Don't worry about them. They are two poor
old blind people; we shared our rice with them tonight."

I walked away; she didn't need help. We did. But why didn't
I ask for her blessing before I left? . . . Old woman, it's you who
is our hope.

And that brings me to my last story, one about an old man
with a weather-beaten face and a craggy jaw. In a serious mood
and with the right hat, he looked like Anthony Quinn; with a
pipe in his hand and a twinkle in his eyes, you'd think of good
Pope John. I speak, of course, of Bishop Fortich.

Bishop Antonio Y. Fortich reached his seventy-fifth birthday on August 11, 1989. Several months later he tendered his resignation to the pope as canon law requires. On the day after his resignation was accepted, the phone rang in the old priests' home where he now lived. It was a long distance call from London. A woman's voice came over the wires: "Is that Bishop Fortich? You have just been nominated for the Nobel Peace Prize."

There were many reasons why Bishop Fortich should be nominated for the Nobel Prize. One of these was his proposal of Peace Zones.

The Peace Zones were not welcome to the military because the proposal seemed to put the beleaguered NPA on the same footing as the military, to give them belligerency status, something no government wants to give to rebels. Neither were the NPA enthusiastic. But while the NPA remained silent, the military was wrathful at the proposals. If the members of the military had thought a little, they would have seen that in some ways the Peace Zone would be more of a disadvantage to the NPA than to themselves. The guerrillas would be stopped from patrolling at night in some places where the military on their own could never stop them.

With all this in the air, the priests of Negros proposed a Peace Caravan around the coast road that encircles Negros to promote the idea of peace—the caravan would stop at the major cities of Negros Occidental and Oriental. It would also sidetrack into the mountains to my old parish of Candoni, where it would witness the setting up of a Peace Zone in the little hamlet of Cantomanyog, where Bishop Fortich, with the help of Fr. Luis Jalandoni, had started a community farm twenty years before. The plan for the Peace Zone had come from the people themselves; they had heard of Bishop Fortich's proposal and that it was backed by Cory Aquino. Their plans were seconded by Fr. Rolex Nueva, the young parish priest of Candoni, who himself was a member of the international Catholic peace organization Pax Christi.

The Peace Caravan set off on February 13, 1990 after a Mass

at Queen of Peace Church said by the new bishop, Camilo Gregorio.

The tour around the island was almost complete, and I drove ahead of the caravan to be in the Peace Zone early.

When I got to Candoni, Bishop Fortich was there already. He sat in the *sala* of the *convento* with Fr. Rolex and some of the other early arrivals. He was worried. Fr. Rolex was explaining that he had just come in from the road leading to the planned Peace Zone; it was blocked by a crowd of four hundred people led by an ex-NPA member. He wore dark glasses and a mask and controlled the crowd with a bullhorn. They were screaming, "We don't want your Peace Zone."

We were all deeply disturbed at the news. Everything had been prepared at the zone site — the altar and all the Mass vessels, the food for hundreds of people soon to arrive with the Peace Caravan. What were the people of Cantomanyog, locked inside the Peace Zone, feeling now? And who were these people blocking the way? They seemed to have appeared from nowhere; they were certainly not from Cantomanyog.

We decided on a Plan A and a Plan B. Plan A was the original plan, saying Mass at the Peace Zone site in Cantomanyog and inaugurating it there. Plan B was this: If we could not pass the barricade, we would say Mass exactly there where we were stopped and inaugurate the Peace Zone from there. We had done our best, and we would leave the rest to God.

Suddenly we heard a sound like high-pitched machine guns; it was a helicopter gunship approaching. We looked out the window to see General Raymundo Jarque, army commander of Negros. The bishop told Fr. Rolex to go straight down, greet them and invite them up. From under the table he pulled a couple of baskets of sandwiches and eggs and pushed them toward me. "These are for the soldiers," he said. Soon Jarque arrived at the *convento* with a bevy of soldiers in fatigues and armed with M16 assault rifles.

Fortich stood up and welcomed them. Then he indicated to me and some others to start distributing the eggs and sandwiches. At first I was somewhat reluctant, but as I went from soldier to soldier, as their faces cracked into smiles, I also found myself smiling and the tension easing. Only when the soldiers and General Jarque and his aides had eaten and drunk did Fortich allow serious talk to begin.

General Jarque said that the peace zone would endanger Philippine sovereignty because the government writ would not run there. "Not at all," said Fortich. "In fact, it is the opposite." He explained that peace would be restored so that for the first time in a long time government services could be delivered; the mayor himself would be fully in charge of the whole thing. The mayor sat silent on a chair, obviously not prepared to say anything that would disturb Jarque.

Then Jarque took up the *Daily Star* newspaper and showed Fortich where it said that this Peace Zone would be monitored by the NPA and the military. He did not like that; it seemed to put the NPA on the same footing as the military.

Fortich said that these were mere details—there was no need for that monitoring. The basic thing the people were asking was that the NPA and the military would not enter with guns into that tiny area. "If you must fight," the bishop said with a twinkle, "please do so outside the Peace Zone."

Now about the blockade—would Jarque lift it? Then Jarque explained without batting an eyelid that the blockade had nothing to do with him. He said that it was the citizens who had raised the barricade, but that maybe Bishop Fortich could go out and dialogue with them?

As I listened I felt misgivings. Would an old campaigner like Fortich fall for that? What dialogue could there be with a trained screaming mob? But Fortich agreed, and since the caravan had not yet arrived, we felt it was best to go immediately up the road to the barricade so that things could be settled before the caravan arrived. We wanted to avoid a confrontation, and those in the caravan might feel angry; especially after a long five-day trek.

I was a little delayed in going out to the barricade. Bishop Fortich and Fr. Rolex and the mayor went ahead. I was horrified when I arrived to find Bishop Fortich actually addressing the crowd, looking up at them where they had massed at a narrow point on the road as it sloped upward on its way to Cantomanyog.

As he spoke, the leader of the crowd—the man with the purple glasses and Balaklava mask—heckled and shouted and led a trained group among the crowd in ridiculing him. Quietly, amid the heckling, the bishop explained the meaning of the Peace Zone. But the leader kept shouting back. I don't know how the bishop felt, but I was mortified for him. He was one of the few on this island who had ever really done anything for the poor and particularly for these mountain people. Now he was being despised and rejected publicly. Such was the pain I felt that for the first time I realized I loved the old man. Eventually, as he was still being shouted down, the bishop lowered his head and stepped back quietly and withdrew to the side.

Then Fr. Rolex asked to speak. "May I have the horn?" "Will we give him the horn?" shouted the masked man. "No," shouted the group within the group. Then the masked man shouted again: "Don't try to deceive us using the name of God to preach violence." But Fr. Rolex continued to speak. "When I said Mass among you, did I ever preach violence?" A silence fell for a moment. "When I said Mass among you, did I not ask you to help one another?" Silence. But the leader started shouting again. Finally Rolex said: "I am inviting you to join our Mass, which we will celebrate over here." So it was to be Plan B.

We got a small table from one of the houses, and Rolex produced a chalice with bread and wine. The bishop vested and so did those priests who were present. Just then over the hill appeared the caravan, now grown to some forty vehicles, each containing about ten people. Not sure of what was happening, they jumped out of the jeepneys. Some thirty priests were among them. All were confused at the sight of the obviously hostile crowd on the hill blocking the way. But they could see us vesting for the Mass. So, they took out their cassocks and joined us. They had a portable sound system, and they gave the microphone to Bishop Fortich at the makeshift altar. Then the Mass began.

During the encounter between the bishop, Fr. Rolex and the crowd, we had had some time to assess what was happening. The crowd had been brought in from two other municipalities — Cauayan and Sipalay. They had been trained by a captain from the army, the same captain who had wanted my friend, the nurse, shot. Jarque was behind this. There were also some people from the nearby barrio of Haba. The military, during the week before, had gone house by house at Haba and got some of the people to join the barricade. Ironically, their reason for joining, apart from fear, was that some of them were annoyed because their barrio had *not* been included in the Peace Zone! Others had had a relative killed by the NPA, so were vulnerable to the military propaganda. Looking at the barricade, it was clear that the heckling came from a small group strategically placed within the larger group.

Behind the barricade was a row of military in fatigues carrying machine guns. The line stretched so that if a person wished to cross the fields to either side of the barricade he or she could be stopped by these soldiers. Thus the people of Cantomanyog were isolated from us completely.

The Mass was now underway. The bishop started with the words "The Lord be with you." I heard the masked man shout, "The Lord is with us — we are all priests." But after that, gradually, the voices died down. A disagreement seemed to be building among those at the barricade. As the Mass advanced, some people — probably those from Haba — began to trickle over to the Mass site. By the time Bishop Fortich began his sermon, a silence had fallen over the barricade crowd. The masked man had given up shouting. By the time the bishop raised the host, total silence reigned over the two congregations. From the angle where I stood I could see Fr. Rolex with his hand over his eyes. Two steady streams of tears flowed nonstop down his face.

Then, at the kiss of peace, something happened. Without us noticing, the people from Cantomanyog — the very people who were blocked off from us by the barricade — had braved their way through and past the barricade and slipped into the crowd at the Mass. When the kiss of peace came, there was a terrible

commotion because when Fr. Rolex recognized them they all began to cry and Fr. Rolex himself broke down completely. In fact, almost everyone at the Mass had wet eyes at this stage.

After communion Fr. Rolex called the people of Cantomanyog to the microphone and a young woman stepped forward holding a little baby. Behind her stood other women, some widows in black, and some men, all victims of the war raking the mountains, all forced to evacuate from their homes at one time or another.

Fr. Rolex stood behind the young woman. She stood before the altar holding her little child on her right arm and the microphone in her free hand. Opposite her, on the hill, in hearing distance, were the remaining people in the barricade.

Behind them, stretched out in a row, were the heavily armed soldiers. In a clear voice she announced the setting up of the Peace Zone — the first Peace Zone in Negros. With a lump in my throat, I crouched forward and took a photograph: A mother and child announcing tidings of hope.

Notes

1. Island of Tears

1. O'Brien, *Revolution from the Heart*, pp. 40ff.

2. *Hacenderos* who have tried to change the system include Ernie Abaya, Susan Abong, Baging Arguelles, Fred Elizalde, Nena and Nene Garcia, Carmen Gamboa, Mario Gonzaga, Carlos Hilado, Ignacio and Nena Javellana (the famous Katilingban Sta. Catalina-Tuburan Model), Cristina Lacson, former governor Daniel Lacson, Oscar Ledesma, Eduardo and Jeanette Locsin (Chito Foundation), former senator Dr. Jose C. Locsin, Sonny Ng, the Soriano and Jalandoni families of La Castellana.

3. In 1988 the poverty threshold in the Western Visayas region stood at $105.80 a month. Granted that the minimum wage was paid in full every day without the mandatory deductions, the monthly take of the workers in such a hacienda would amount only to $80.40, well below the poverty threshold. Since there is no work during the off season, the yearly wage divided by twelve shows a monthly income forty percent (40%) less again (*Philippine Statistical Yearbook 1990*, Table 2-10, p. 2-21).

4. When asked about the actual number of planters who subjected their farms to the 60-30-10 voluntary land sharing and transfer scheme, Dr. Violeta Lopez-Gonzaga, the province's foremost expert on agrarian reform, remarked: "You can count on your fingers the planters who have subjected their farms to the 60-30-10 land sharing scheme" (25 June 1992).

5. For a three-year period (January 1989 to January 1992), 1,149 haciendas were inspected by a government labor monitoring body. The inspection showed that 50% of the haciendas visited were not paying the minimum wage ("349 Farms Violate Labor Laws," *Visayan Daily Star*, 12 June 1992, p. 1).

6. In a forum entitled, "The Sugar Industry: Retrospect and Prospect," Governor Rafael Coscolluela, in reply to a question of a student

217

about the future of the province in the light of the planned liberalization of sugar importation, said: "I dream of the day when sugar is gone but all of us are flourishing. In its present state, the sugar industry will never solve our poverty problem" (University of St. La Salle, 28 July 1992).

7. Robert Fogel, *Without Consent or Contract*, as quoted in a BBC broadcast, September 1990.

8. McCoy and de Jesus, eds., *Philippine Social History*, pp. 320, 322.

9. Robert Tabor, *War of the Flea* (New York: L. Stuart, 1965).

10. Thirty-five thousand people left their homes and lands because of operations Thunderbolt, Amihan, and Habagat ("Thunderbolt Ends; Rehab Plan Readied," *Visayan Daily Star*, 6 June 1989, p. 1).

11. Despite the hundreds of children who perished because of Operation Thunderbolt, a newspaper columnist wrote that "such sacrifice would be worth all the trouble . . . if the . . . military operations would eventually restore peace and quiet in strife-torn . . . villages" ("Evacuees," *Visayan Daily Star*, 12 May 1989, p. 3).

12. A newspaper columnist reduced the possible attitudes toward Operation Thunderbolt to two: either for the military or for the NPA. "There is no middle ground," he said ("Conflict," *Visayan Daily Star*, June 28, 1989, p. 3 col. 5 to p. 6, cols. 1 and 2).

13. I received this account from Maryknoll Father Tom Marti, who attended the meeting with President Aquino on July 7, 1988.

14. Subsequently these government officials organized a "people's demonstration" (using the military) against the parish priest of Himamaylan and the Presentation sisters working there, accusing them of being communists ("Church Groups Hit Rally," *Visayan Daily Star*, 22 August 1990, pp. 1-2).

15. a) Contrary to popular belief that Negros was economically backward prior to the introduction of sugar, Violeta Lopez-Gonzaga wrote that in the mid-nineteenth century the island had a thriving subsistence economy producing rice and corn sufficient for daily needs (Violeta Lopez-Gonzaga, *Capital Expansion, Frontier Development, and the Rise of the Monocrop Economy in Negros (1850-1898)*, Occasional Paper No. 1, [Bacolod City: La Salle Social Research-Negrense Studies' Program, 1987]).

b) According to Alcalde Mayor Jose Saenz de Vizmanos, the free upland Malay people were better off than their lowland counterparts. The former were better fed and had sturdier dwellings. In times of famine, lowlanders would flee to the mountains for subsistence (Hernaez Romero, p. 64).

16. McCoy and de Jesus, eds., *Philippine Social History*, p. 306.

17. McCoy, *Priests on Trial*, p. 76.

18. The bitter consequences are manifold. To name only a few:
1) Landlessness: In a predominantly agricultural province, 41% of Negros Occidental households do not have land (Violeta Lopez-Gonzaga, Virgilio Aguilar, and Ferris Fe Demegillo, *Resource Base for Agrarian Reform and Development in Negros Occidental* [Bacolod City: Institute for Social Research and Development, 1988], pp. 7-8).

2) Concentration of sugar lands in the hands of a minority: 21 percent of sugar landowners control 80 percent of the total land area planted to sugar (Gonzaga, Aguilar, and Demegillo, p. 42).

3) Poverty: Landless sugar workers ranked first among seven poverty groups identified in a study made in 1983 (Felomino Aguilar, Jr., p. 18).

19. Land area planted to sugar comprises 64.57 percent of the total agricultural land of the province; land area planted to rice comprises 12 percent (Gonzaga, Aguilar, and Demegillo, p. 4).

20. A Swedish Space Company's satellite survey shows 50 percent of the province's land has been eroded.

21. Only 6 percent of the coral reefs in Western Negros can be considered in excellent condition.

22. The Department of Environment and Natural Resources estimates that 32,500 acres of mangrove in the province have been converted into fishponds and prawn farms, leaving only 1,200 acres of mangrove forests.

23. O'Brien, *Revolution from the Heart*, pp. 31-32.

24. See the writings of Dr. Violeta Lopez-Gonzaga, University of St. La Salle; Dr. Alfred W. McCoy, University of Wisconsin at Madison; Dr. Michael Billig, Franklin and Marshall College; and Dr. Rosanne Rutten, University of Amsterdam.

25. Hobhouse, *Seeds of Change*, pp. 45ff.

26. The collusion of the landlords and the military is exemplified by the use of the so-called Sugar Development Fund (SDF). The SDF was formed out of the contributions of individual planters. A portion of it was — and still is at time of writing — being allocated for the allowances, benefits, armaments, and supplies of Citizen's Armed Forces Geographical Unit (CAFGU) companies in Negros Occidental. In exchange, the CAFGUs provide security in and around the landlords' sugar plantations. CAFGUs are paramilitary forces established by the AFP during the Aquino administration to combat the New Peoples Army (NPA). The CAFGUs are notorious locally and internationally for human rights abuses ("Negros Landlords Cut CAFGU Subsidy," *Manila Chronicle*, 18 March 1991, n. p.).

27. As a reaction to the prospective Comprehensive Agrarian Reform Law, rightist planters formed the Movement for an Independent Negros (MIN) and started building up a stockpile of arms for a planned secessionist revolt (McCoy, "The Restoration of Planter Power in La Carlota City," p. 128), where he names the planters. Since this publication his life has been threatened.

2. Where Does the Church Stand?

1. Interview with Bishop Emeritus Fortich, July 1992.
2. It has been pointed out to me that the Soviet Union did collapse a few months after the pope and the bishops consecrated Russia to Mary, Theotokos, the Mother of God. I believe these acts of faith are significant, but my point here is that the serious concern for the spiritual welfare of far-away Russia was accompanied by a lack of feeling for great suffering going on close at home. Genuine devotion to Mary, the prophet of the Magnificat, will be accompanied by compassion for the hacienda workers and zeal to better their lot.

3. Armed Struggle

1. O'Brien, *Seeds of Injustice*, pp. 103-106.
2. Fr. Edgar Saguinsin was later forced to leave the Philippines because of threats to his life arising from this work; Fr. Hector Mauri came to Negros in the 1950s to try to do something about the plantations. He failed, but in spite of recurring heart attacks he kept up his agitation for the workers into his 80s.
3. Hernaez Romero, pp. 104ff.
4. Hernaez Romero, p. 134.
5. This is corroborated by the action of the Negrense elite during the period immediately following the end of the Spanish regime; they granted full citizenship in the short-lived federal government only to those with land and capital (Violeta Lopez-Gonzaga, *The Socio-Politics of Sugar*, p. 9).
6. McSorley, p. 81.
7. LeRoy Walters, *Five Classic Just-War Theories* (New Haven, Connecticut: Yale University Press, 1971), p. 85.
8. Dorr, p. 148.
9. Some of the priests killed: Zacharias Agatep, Pites Bernardo, Tullio Favali, Rudy Romano, Nilo Valerio, Nerilito Satur, Narciso Pico

P.I.C., Salvatore Carzedda, Carl Schmitz. Some of these were also tortured.

4. Silence

1. They did move later, over their own wages and conditions, but never significantly against the prostitution of the educational system in the service of the martial law ideology.
2. Sharp, *The Politics of Nonviolent Action*, p. 88.
3. They were victimized during the Marcos years, a) by the sugar monopoly, NASUTRA, and PHILSUCOM of Roberto S. Benedicto; b) by the sugar mills over their fair share of the sugar.
4. Regalado, Aurora Alarde, *Barriers in the Development of the Philippine Sugar Industry* (Philippine Peasant Institute, Milan, 1992), p. 27, Table 10.
5. Etienne La Boetie, quoted in Sharp, *The Politics of Nonviolent Action*, p. 34.
6. Sharp, *Gandhi as a Political Strategist*, p. 54.
7. Sharp, *The Politics of Nonviolent Action*, p. 9.

5. The Spurious Choice

1. Wink, pp. 13-14.
2. Hildegard and Jean Goss-Mayr. This expression was a constant refrain of the late Jean Goss-Mayr in the seminars he gave in the Philippines and throughout the world.
3. *Christian Community Bible.* The ideas in these pages are partly taken from the CCB's commentary on Matthew's Sermon on the Mount.

6. Active Nonviolence

1. M. K. Gandhi, *All Men are Brothers* (New York: Columbia University Press, 1989), p. 101-2.
2. O'Brien, *Revolution from the Heart*, p. 120.
3. Wink, p. 6.
4. Earl and Pat Hostetters, "First World Pacifism and Third World Violence," *Sojourners* (April 1983). The U. S. bases have since gone.

5. Jean and Hildegard Goss-Mayr, p. 27.

6. Madonna Kolbenschlag, talk given in Washington, D. C., November 1986.

7. Sharp, *Making Europe Unconquerable*, pp. 127ff.

8. Adolf Hitler, quoted in Sharp, *The Politics of Nonviolent Action*, p. 46.

9. Sharp, *The Politics of Nonviolent Action*.

10. Ibid., p. 121.

11. Ibid., pp. 89-90.

12. Gaspar, pp. 15ff.

13. After the collapse of East Germany, evidence appeared that Libya was not involved this time.

14. Lovett, p. 13.

15. Sharp, *Gandhi as a Political Strategist*, pp. 31-32.

7. Does It Work?

1. O'Brien, *Revolution from the Heart*, p. 214.

2. Jawarhalal Nehru, quoted in Sharp, *Politics of Nonviolent Action*, p. 87.

3. Some of those who died working with NAMFREL: Jaime Alcala, Hamlet Canales, Fructuoso Tavines, Ireneo Magbanua, Samuel Montes, Alexis Parao, Rodrigo Ponce, Dan Sarmiento (Byington, pp. 187ff. and dedication page).

4. Martin Buber, quoted in Estey and Hunter, pp. 146-47.

5. Virgilio Aguilar, *"The Process of Agrarian Reform Implementation in Negros Occidental,"* ed. Atty. Raymundo Pandan, ISRAD Research Notes Series No. 4 (Bacolod City: Institute for Social Research and Development, 1991), pp. 18ff.

6. McCoy, "The Restoration of Planter Power in La Carlota City," pp. 105-34.

7. The 1992 elections were an improvement on previous ones but careful inquiries done on several haciendas showed that laborers were still controlled (McCoy, "The Restoration of Planter Power in La Carlota City").

8. Negros

1. Galileo Kintanar, quoted in McCoy, *Priests on Trial*, p. 202.

2. "Thousands Evacuated in Negros," *Manila Chronicle*, 13 May 1989.

3. *Acts and Decrees of the Second Plenary Council of the Philippines*, Article 140 (Manila: Catholic Bishops' Conference of the Philippines, 1992).

9. Reconciliation

1. J. Cabazares, "Toward Peace Building." Extract from his poem "Reconciliation: A Return to the God of Peace" as it appeared in *Towards Peace Building, an Anthology*, Nagliliyab Series (Quezon City: Claretian Publications, 1987), pp. 5-6.

2. O'Brien, *Seeds of Injustice*, p. 165.

10. Forgiveness

1. Allan Berlow obtained that report and gave me a xerox copy of it. It is dated 10 April 1988. Section V (a) reads: "Recommend that awards be given to the personnel involved in the encounter." It is signed: Allan Arrojado, 1st Lieutenant, (INP) Pa, Officer-in-charge.

11. Stumbling Blocks

1. List of planters who presented the plaque: Bob Jalandoni, Antonio Sian, Anne Ledesma, Luis and Betty de la Rama, Jose Ma. and Ludy Lacson, Jr., Amalia Unson, Antonio and Gloria Esteban, Ignacio and Sylvia Javellana, Beny Ortaliz, Hernando and Aida Abaya, Gina Bautista, Rafael and Baby Golez, Ricardo C. Silverio, Cano and Susan Villarosa, Nani E. Jiminez, Roy, Ruska and Ryan Gamboa, Yen and Min Gaston and Family, Maia V. Ramos, Nestor Jalandoni, Sergie and Menchi Tan, Arvi and Cecile Javelona, Johnny and Miriam Tagamolila, Lydia Lizares, Mayor Alfredo Montelibano, Jr., Nani and Tata Millan, Lourdes Fernandez, Chuchu and Inday Kramer, Egbert and Laura Alarcon, Ma. Milagros M. Benedicto, Carmen Legaspi, Baging and Lyn Arguelles, Tess A. Gaston, and Medy Garcia.

2. Albert Nolan, *Taking Sides*, p. 5. An essay appearing in *Liberation Theology and the Vatican Document*, Vol. 3, Quezon City: Claretian Publicatiions, 1987.

3. "Editorial," *Visayan Daily Star*, 6 July 1989, p. 3.

4. Wink, p 7.

13. Suffering

1. Lovett, p. 13.
2. Daniel Berrigan, "A Servant Song of Justice," *Sojourners* (July 1989).

15. Spirituality in a Revolutionary Situation

1. Albert Nolan, *Jesus Before Christianity* (Maryknoll, New York: Orbis Books, 1978).
2. Alfred McCoy, "Inside the RAM," February 1990, *Philippine Daily Inquirer*, Special Issue.
3. "Junior Military Official Airs Frustrations," *Panay News*, 3-4 April 1991.
4. One example is the alleged purge of 800 cadres from the ranks in Davao in the mid-1980s as related by Jose Ma. Sison, founder of the Communist Party of the Philippines (CCP), in his FAX message to the *Philippine Daily Inquirer*, December 17, 1992. In the ensuing debate between party members carried on through the pages of the *Philippine Daily Inquirer* that month, top party officials acknowledged that the said cadres had been killed and, in many cases, tortured too.
5. Bertolt Brecht as quoted in Lovett, *Life Before Death* (Quezon City: Claretian Publications, 1986), p. 59.
6. Myers, p. 189.

Epilogue

1. "At the first Mass for the Alvarados and Antonio Alisbo, the carpenter, one of the concelebrants said, 'Perhaps the offering of these six lives will call attention to the iniquitous situation here, where people try to build tiny houses and squat on the fringes of the city, in fact on the old city dump, and are being forcibly driven off by those who have occupied most of the rest of the land in Negros, by means of the National Security Forces in the pay of the wealthy' " (Brendan O'Connell, *Columban Mission*, Nebraska, October 1991).

Aileen was pregnant at the time of the massacre. A couple of days later she gave birth. In the chaotic condition of the family the new baby soon contracted pneumonia. Noel had to sell his boat to pay the hospital expenses: in vain because the baby died. Noel now hires himself out on the boats of others.

The case caused special scandal for another reason. An editorial in the *Visayan Daily Star*, 31 July 1992, eighteen months later, commenting on their own report that those accused of the massacre were leaving the jail at will, without bail, said: "The Magsungay massacre, which happened May 5 last year, was one of the bloodiest and most sensational cases ever to hit Bacolod in many years. Six persons were killed, including a one-year-old child. If the process of justice in such a case could be characterized by such casualness, what can we expect about other less publicized crimes?" The casualness refers to the fact that the accused were not living in the jail. They were only locked up again through the pressure caused by reporter Carla Gomez's investigative reporting in the *Visayan Daily Star.*

Selected Bibliography

Aguilar, Felomeno V., Jr. *The Making of Cane Sugar: Poverty, Crisis, and Change in Negros Occidental.* Bacolod City: La Salle Social Research Center, 1984.

Billig, Michael. "Syrup in the Wheels of Progress: The Inefficient Organization of the Philippine Sugar Industry." Unpublished paper, 1992.

Byington, Kaa. *Bantay ng Bayan.* Manila: Bookmark, 1988.

Canlas, Mamerto, Mariano Miranda, Jr., and James Putzel. *Land, Poverty and Politics in the Philippines.* Quezon City: Claretian Publications, 1988.

Christian Community Bible. Quezon City: Claretian/St. Paul/Divine Word Publications, 1988.

Claver, Francisco F., SJ. "Nonviolence: The Imperative of Faith?" Unpublished lecture.

Coblentz, Stanton A. *From Arrow to Atom Bomb: The Psychological History of War.* New York: Beechhurst Press, 1953.

Connon, F. *Missing: Fr. Rudy Romano.* Cebu: Redemptorist Justice and Peace Desk, 1987.

Coote, Belinda. *The Hunger Crop.* Oxford: Oxfam, 1987.

Cornell, Thomas C., and James H. Forest, eds. *A Penny a Copy: Readings from the Catholic Worker.* New York: Macmillan, 1969.

Coronel, Miguel. *Pro-Democracy People's War.* Quezon City: Vanmarc Ventures, 1991.

Cullman, Oscar. *Jesus and the Revolutionaries.* New York: Harper & Row, 1970.

de Achutegui, Pedro S., SJ. *John Paul II in the Philippines: Addresses and Homilies.* Quezon City: Ateneo de Manila University, 1981.

Dorr, Donal. *Option for the Poor: A Hundred Years of Vatican Social Teaching.* Dublin: Gill & Macmillan; and Maryknoll, N.Y.: Orbis Books, 1983; revised edition, 1992.

Estey, George, and Doris Hunter. *Nonviolence: A Reader in the Ethics of Action.* Waltham, Mass.: Xerox College Publishing, 1971.

Fackenheim, Emil L. *God's Presence in History: Jewish Affirmations and Philosophical Reflections.* New York: Harper & Row, 1970.

Forest, Jim, and Nancy Forest. *Four Days in February.* London: Marshall Pickering, 1988.

Gaspar, Karl M., CSSR. *A People's Option: To Struggle for Creation.* Quezon City: Claretian Publications, 1990.

Geremia, Peter, PIME, ed. *Church Persecution.* Quezon City: Claretian Publications, 1988.

Goss-Mayr, Jean, and Hildegard Goss-Mayr. *The Gospel and the Struggle for Peace.* Alkmaar: International Fellowship of Reconciliation, 1990.

Graham, Helen R., MM. *You Will Be Handed Over.* Quezon City: Claretian Publications, 1987.

Gremillion, Joseph, ed. *The Gospel of Peace and Justice: Catholic Social Teaching Since Pope John.* Maryknoll, N.Y.: Orbis Books, 1975.

Haring, Bernard, CSSR. *Healing and Revealing.* Slough, England: St. Paul Publications, 1984.

Hernaez Romero, Marie Fe. *Negros Occidental: Between Two Foreign Powers.* Bacolod City: Negros Historical Commission, 1974.

Hendrickx, Herman. *Peace Anyone?* Quezon City: Claretian Publications, 1986.

Hobhouse, Henry. *Seeds of Change.* New York: Perennial Library, 1987.

Holland, Joe, and Peter Henriot, SJ. *Social Analysis: Linking Faith and Justice.* Maryknoll, N.Y.: Orbis Books, 1985.

Houver, Gerard. *A Non-Violent Lifestyle.* London: Marshall Morgan and Scott/Lamp Press, 1989.

Jecena, Arsenio, SJ. "The Sacadas of Sugarland," in *Liberation in Sugarland.* Manila: Kibapil, 1971.

Las Casas, Bartolome de. *In Defense of the Indians,* translated by Stafford Poole, CM. Dekalb, Ill.: Northern Illinois University Press, 1967.

Ledesma, Antonio J., SJ, and Ma. Lourdes T. Montinoloa. *The Implementation of Agrarian Reform in Negros.* Bacolod City: The Social Research Center, 1988.

Liberation Theology and the Vatican Document, vol. 2. Quezon City: Claretian Publications, 1986.

Liberation Theology and the Vatican Document, vol. 3. Quezon City: Claretian Publications, 1987.

Lopez-Gonzaga, Violeta B. *The Sacadas in Negros: Poverty Profile.* Bacolod City: La Salle Social Research Center, 1984.

———. *Crisis and Poverty in Sugarlandia: The Case of Bacolod.* Bacolod City: La Salle Social Research Center, 1985.

————. *The Socio-Politics of Sugar: Wealth, Power Formation and Change in Negros (1899-1985)*. Bacolod City: The Social Research Center, 1989.

————. *The Negrense: A Social History of an Elite Class*. Bacolod: Institute for Social Research and Development, 1991.

————. *Land of Plenty, Land of Want: A Socio-Economic History of Negros* (1571-1985). Unpublished ms.

Lovett, Brendan. *On Earth as in Heaven: Corresponding to God in Philippine Context*. Quezon City: Claretian Publications, 1988.

Lynch, Frank, SJ. *A Bittersweet Taste of Sugar*. Quezon City: Ateneo de Manila University Press, 1970.

Manapat, Ricardo. *Some Are Smarter Than Others*. New York: Aletheia Publications, 1991.

Martinez Cuesta, Angel, OAR. *Historia de la Isla de Negros, Filipinas: 1565-1896*. Madrid: Raycar, S.A., 1974.

McCoy, Alfred W. "Baylan: Animist Religion and Philippines Peasant Ideology." Manila: *Philippine Quarterly of Society and Culture*, 1983.

————. *Priests on Trial*. Victoria, Australia: Penguin, 1984.

————. "The Restoration of Planter Power in La Carlota City," in *From Marcos to Aquino: Local Perspectives on the Political Transition in the Philippines*, ed. Benedict Kerkvliet and Resil B. Majores. Quezon City: Ateneo de Manila University Press, 1991.

McCoy, Alfred W., and Ed C. de Jesus, eds. *Philippine Social History*. Honolulu: University Press of Hawaii, 1982.

McSorley, Richard. *New Testament Basis of Peacemaking*. Scottdale, Penn.: Herald Press, 1979.

Merton, Thomas. *Faith and Violence*. South Bend, Ind.: Notre Dame University Press, 1965.

Munro, Ross H. "The New Khmer Rouge." *Commentary*, December 1985.

Musto, Ronald G. *The Catholic Peace Tradition*. Maryknoll, N.Y.: Orbis Books, 1986.

Myers, Ched. *Binding the Strong Man: A Political Reading of Mark's Story of Jesus*. Maryknoll, N.Y.: Orbis Books, 1988.

O'Brien, Niall. *Revolution from the Heart*. Quezon City: Claretian Publications, 1988; New York: Oxford University Press, 1987; Maryknoll, N.Y.: Orbis Books, 1991.

————. *Seeds of Injustice*. Dublin: O'Brien Press, 1985.

Pimentel, Benjamin, Jr. *EDJOP: The Unusual Journey of Edgar Jopson*. Quezon City: Ken Inc., 1989.

Primer: Basic Christian Community. Bacolod Diocesan Pastoral Center, 1989.

Rutten, Rosanne. *Women Workers of Hacienda Milagros*. Amsterdam: Publikatieserie Zuid-en Zuidoost-Azie, 1982.

Sa-onoy, Modesto P. *A History of Negros Occidental*. Bacolod City: Today Printers and Publishers, 1992.

Scott, William Henry. *Cracks in the Parchment Curtain and Other Essays in the Philippine History*. Quezon City: New Day Publishers, 1982.

Sharp, Gene. *Social Power and Political Freedom*. Boston: Porter Sargent Publishers, 1980.

————. *Making Europe Unconquerable*. Cambridge, Mass.: Ballinger Publishing Co., 1985.

————. *The Politics of Nonviolent Action*, 3 vols. Boston: Porter Sargent Publishers, 1973.

————. *Gandhi as a Political Strategist*. Boston: Porter Sargent Publishers, 1979.

Sivard, Ruth Leger. *World Military and Social Expenditures 1985*. Washington, DC: World Priorities, 1985.

Stannard, Bruce. *Poor Man's Priest*. Sydney: Collins/Fontana, 1984.

"The Sugar Workers of Negros." A Study Commissioned by the Association of Major Religious Superiors in the Philippines. Columban Fathers, Manila n.d.

Tison, Ma. Lourdes M., and Simon Peter Gregorio. *Beyond the Barricade: Sitio Cantomanyog and Its Struggle for Peace*. Bacolod City: Paghiliusa sa Paghida-et, 1992.

Topel, L. John, SJ. *The Way to Peace*. Maryknoll, N.Y.: Orbis Books, 1979.

True, Michael. *Justice Seekers, Peace Makers*. Mystic, Conn.: Twenty-Third Publications, 1985.

Vanderhaar, Gerard. *Nonviolence in Christian Tradition*. London: Pax Christi, 1983.

Vanderhaar, Gerard, and Janice Vanderhaar. *The Philippines: Agony and Hope*. Erie, Penn.: Pax Christi USA, 1989.

Washington, James Melvin, ed. *A Testament of Hope: The Essential Writings of Martin Luther King, Jr.* San Francisco: Harper & Row, 1986.

Wink, Walter. *Violence and Nonviolence in South Africa*. Philadelphia: New Society Publishers, 1987.

Yoder, John H. *What Would You Do?* Scottdale, Penn.: Herald Press, 1983.

Index

231